THE
BEATITUDES
God's Plan For Battle

The Battle Has
Already Begun.

Russell Stendal

THE BEATITUDES

God's Plan For Battle
Russell M. Stendal © 1993

Revised Pocket Edition © 2009

All Scripture references are from
the Jubilee Bible 2000 ©
2001 Russell Martin Stendal

Art work by Osvaldo Lara
Layout by Martha Jaramillo R.

Email: martinstendal@etb.net.co

ISBN 0-931221-41-2
To order more books:
        www.dwightclough.com/books
        Office hours 608-834-8291
To order by mail: Dwight Clough
        1223 West Main Street # 228
        Sun Prairie, Wisconsin 53590 USA

November, 2009
Printed in Colombia

Table of Contents

Dedication

*T*HIS BOOK IS DEDICATED TO MY WIFE, Marina, and the four wonderful children that God has given us. Our marriage (in 1980) marked a water shed in my spiritual life as the Lord used Marina to smooth many rough edges off of me and to place our lives on a steady course towards attaining more and more of His Blessing. She has proven to be a wonderful helpmeet and has had a great impact on the contents of this volume.

The birth of our daughter, Elizabeth Jean, (we call her Lisa) in 1982, marked another turning point in my life. About that time, I began to feel a very strong call of God to walk in victory (with clean hands) before Him. At first It seemed that God was asking me to do the impossible, but from the time of Lisa's birth I felt a renewed sense of God's grace in my life. Elizabeth literally means "to whom God is the oath" in Hebrew and I found, from that time on, that

God really does back up His Word with Himself (with the power of His presence) in the lives of those who take Him seriously.

Sixteen years ago, as I was in a great dilemma trying to name our second daughter (the baby was almost a month old and still didn't have a name!) I felt an impulse to put down the baby name books I had been reading and that I should get out my concordance. I soon found a beautiful name for our lovely girl using the Greek word for truth. The birth of Alethia Joy (meaning the joy of the truth) was a great milestone in my life. The Lord had been teaching me the full meaning of the verse *"... and you shall know the truth, and the truth shall set you free."* As Christians, the truth is our weapon, and if used in submission to the will of God brings great deliverance, victory, and joy.

Ten years ago, the Lord granted me one of the desires deep within my heart, with the birth of Russell Martin Jr. The birth of my son marked the beginning of my putting together the material that has culminated in the writing of this volume. The baby has given my wife and me great joy as he develops by learning to sit, crawl, and talk. When I edited the first edition of this book in 1993 he was learning to walk. The birth of little Russell marked a great change of course in our ministry when for more than seven years we stopped preaching to multitudes to spend quiet time with the Lord. This led to being the editor of over fifty books and two Bible editions (the Reina Valera 2000 in Spanish and its counterpart, the Jubilee Bible in English).

Then, our second son, Dylan Andrew was born two and a half years ago and the Lord put us back into public ministry on the radio and in person (now in a new dimension).

As I have learned more and more about parenting, I have been able to identify a little more with how God the Father feels as He trains and develops us as His sons. As I have learned more and more about being a husband, I have been able to identify a little more with the desire of our Lord Jesus to return for a victorious bride (Church) without spot or wrinkle. For this reason, I also dedicate this book to all the true sons of God who form part of the "bride without spot or wrinkle", for whom our Lord will soon return.

Russell M. Stendal
August, 2002

Introduction

"First the worker, then the work."

By this phrase, Cameron Townsend, "Uncle Cam", the founder of the Wycliffe Bible Translators meant that God wanted to bring Christian workers into a complete consecration to the Lord. Then God could bless and multiply their Christian work, based on the Biblical standard of love — love for the lost and love for other workers. By this, the whole world should know that the workers and the work were of God. (See I John 3:14) The hardest part of this task was to get the worker in the right relationship with the Lord. Then it was a relatively easy matter to add hundreds or even thousands of believers to the Lord.

My wife and I worked hard for many years under the most demanding primitive conditions. The Lord did many wonderful things for us and opened closed doors to the Kogi tribe in northern

Colombia. We endeavored to walk in the Spirit and to be obedient to His will. All of our four children grew up in the nurture and admonition of the Lord, and now with their spouses are serving God in Colombia.

In 1975, after 13 years with the Wycliffe Bible Translators, we left, with the blessing of the director, to work on winning rural Colombians and Indians to the Lord. This was much more complex than we had imagined. It was not hard to bring them to a superficial commitment, but to see real changed lives, as the New Testament talks about, was difficult indeed. We had many disappointments, as even some of our workers did not continue on victoriously. Somehow, imperceptibly, our own consecration began to slip from the 100% commitment and dedication to the Lord with which we had entered Colombia in 1964. Discouragement set in.

But God is faithful and did not leave us in that condition of despair. On August 14, 1983, Russell, our oldest son, was kidnapped by Marxist guerrillas. I received a call from Russell's co-worker in a new Family Reconciliation Ministry. "I'm so sorry to tell you, Chad, that Russell has been kidnapped," he sadly related.

Russell had flown his plane to Caño Jabon, a small town on the edge of the jungle, trying to help the local people set up a fish marketing co-op. Right then, as I finished talking with

Ricardo, the Lord showed me that God had just "called" a missionary to the communist guerrillas.

All his life, Russ had been very active, running about as though he were connected to a high voltage electric line. He seemingly was capable of accomplishing a great many things, but the spiritual results were not commensurate with the amount of physical effort he was expending. He was too busy to take the time in quiet meditation with the Lord so that he might draw close to the heart of God and be more effective.

All of a sudden, as a prisoner in the jungle with a nylon rope around his neck and shoulders, tied to a tree, he had a lot of time to think. The Lord simply sat him down for 142 days and began to teach him the things he needed to know to be completely consecrated to God and to hear His voice.

Meanwhile, the Lord was doing the same with the rest of our family and co-workers. My wife, Patricia, about wore out her knees in prayer. We all covenanted together to walk as close to the Lord as we could, and He brought us all much closer together in love. We trusted that God in His great mercy might hear and answer our prayers for Russell if we met the conditions of James 5:16, *"The effectual prayer of the righteous is very powerful."*

On the other hand, we had to recognize that if God in His infinite wisdom had selected my son to be a martyr, then we would accept His will. Almost all the Apostles gave their lives, and this is the highest honor the Lord can bestow.

Finally, after almost five months, Russell was released. We all discovered that God had done a profound work in each of our lives, perfecting us to a much higher plane than we had ever dreamed of experiencing. The Lord multiplied our ministry a hundredfold. Churches all over Colombia, the United States, and Canada had been praying for Russell's release. Now they opened their doors for ministry. The small Family Reconciliation Ministry grew to be a National Reconciliation Ministry, extending the Gospel to the drug mafia and the guerrillas. Radio ministry began to flourish.

One day I asked the Lord why Russell had received such a great anointing for ministry, and the Lord showed me that He was restoring to the Church a class of anointed preachers called "Confessors". During the great persecution in the days of the early Church, the Lord not only had martyrs, of whom it was often said, "The blood of the martyrs is the seed of the Church," but the Lord also had "Confessors". These were those who had maintained a good testimony under much persecution and torture. They were tried by the fire and found faithful and true. Many were maimed or blinded but did not deny their Lord. After they were proven to be faithful, the Lord ordained their release, and a great unction and power followed their ministry for the rest of their lives.

In the following book, Russell has distilled the most important fruits of the truth the Lord has shown him during the last ten years, starting with those 142 days in the jungle. "First the worker, then the work."

Chad Stendal
Bogotá, Colombia
August, 1993

Preface

*L*ET ME ASK YOU A QUESTION. What section of Scripture is most relevant to your Christian life? Between the Old Testament and the New Testament of the Bible, most of you would probably pick the New Testament. If you were to consider what is the most important part of the New Testament, I think that most Christians would probably single out the four gospels, recognizing that the life, death, resurrection, and ministry of our Lord Jesus Christ is the most important part of the New Testament.

Out of the four gospels, if you were to pick three chapters that sum up, and synthesize the message that Jesus Christ came to leave with us, the Sermon on the Mount is the prime candidate. It has been called at times the Constitution of the Kingdom of God, the Magna Carta of the Christian Church, and the Little Gospel. There have been more books written on the Sermon on the Mount than on any other Scripture text. Entire libraries could be filled. The Sermon on the Mount has challenged Christians ever since it was given. The proclamation of the Beatitudes by Jesus Christ at the beginning of his public ministry marked the climax, or water-shed of moral teaching. After His message of the Kingdom of God, proclaimed both by His lips and through His very life, death, and resurrection; this world has never been the same. Human history was divided in two: before and after Jesus Christ.

The first few times I read the Sermon on the Mount, I sensed that it contained something important; but for many years, Jesus' Beatitudes and His Sermon on the Mount seemed to me as if they had been written in code. I knew they contained something special, but I couldn't put my finger on it. In confirmation class, I was taught the Lord's Prayer, the Beatitudes, and the Ten Commandments, but I couldn't figure out why I had to memorize all these things. It seemed like an unbelievable waste of time. I never really understood the message that God was trying to get across to me, as I'm sure many of the thousands and thousands of young people who have been forced to memorize the same things never really realized what was behind it.

One day I was driving up the road from Miami to Minneapolis. As we were going through Chattanooga, Tennessee, I turned on the radio and got a preacher I didn't know, but what he said stuck in my mind. He said, "How in the world can we expect to have a deep revival when we are dealing with such a superficial generation?" Do you want a deep revival? Would you like to see a deep revival? Would you really like to see the power of God move in our present society?

Well then, we are going to have to search for God. We are going to have to uncover our hearts before Him. We are going to have to seek Him in a very deep and profound way. God will not give His valuable treasures and powerful gifts to people who just want to be mediocre, superficial Christians, to people who are just trying to see what is the minimum they can do and still go to heaven. That's a terrible position to be in. God is looking for people who will seek Him in spirit and in truth, and who are willing to go His way no matter what.

The great heroes of the faith all went through trials and tribulations. God told Abraham to leave his family, friends, and home town and travel to a land that God promised to give him. After Abraham obeyed, God promised him a son, an heir, through whom all the families of the earth would be blessed (see Genesis 12:2). Twelve years after the miraculous birth of Isaac in his old age, Abraham was called upon by God to sacrifice his son who was most dear to him. When Abraham passed that test, the Bible says that Abraham believed God, and it was counted to him as righteousness, and that Abraham is the father of those who have **faith**. Faith (believing God) is closely linked to **obedience** in the Scriptures. ***If we truly believe God, then we should also be willing to obey Him. If you don't desire to obey God, you really shouldn't read any further in this book about the Beatitudes of the Sermon on the Mount.***

I say this because I don't want to end up having a part in bringing someone under worse condemnation than they already deserve. If you are not going to act on revelation of truth, it might be better for you not to know any more about it, because then your responsibility will be less. If you listen to the Sermon on the Mount and begin to understand Jesus' message, and do not apply it and begin to practice it, and do not seek to implement it into your life; then there is a great and grave responsibility that comes with refusing to act on your knowledge of revealed truth.

Jesus' ministry was preceded by John the Baptist, who was a typical prophet in many ways, but not typical of many preachers today. He preached a very simple message, and it was this: repent and prepare the way for the coming of the Lord. If you are truly repentant, your life should change, and there should be visible fruits of repentance. John said that the axe has been laid to the root of the tree. (see Matthew 3:1-11) Time is running out; judgement is at hand. That was what it was for the Jews, the ones who rejected this message; those who rejected Jesus, whom John the Baptist was announcing. They didn't have very long to wait before their entire nation was uprooted and destroyed and the survivors dispersed all over the known world.

John the Baptist was heralding the end of the age of the Old Testament (the old covenant), the end of the worship in the temple at Jerusalem. A new age, the age of the church, was dawning. In this age, God promised to live in a temple not built with human hands. **God's temple is now us, His people.**

"Know ye not that ye are the temple of God and that

*the Spirit of God dwells in you? If anyone defiles the
temple of God, God shall destroy that one: for the
temple of God is holy, which temple ye are."*
(I Corinthians 3:16,17)

I am convinced that we are now drawing near
to the end of the age of the church. The city of
Jerusalem is once again in the hands of the Jews
after almost two thousand years of being trampled
by the Gentiles (Luke 21:24). Our Lord Jesus Christ's
return is getting closer and closer. God is getting
ready to move again and do something special,
something new. He desires to raise up a people, a
victorious people who have washed their robes in
the blood of the Lamb, that have left their own plans
and ambitions to one side and have become willing
to do things His way, no matter what the cost.

***There is a cost involved in following the
Lord; but it is a price that we must pay voluntarily, of our own free will.*** Jesus is not a
terrorist. He's not like the communist guerrillas I
met who point machine guns at people in order to
get them to do what they want. He doesn't do things
that way. If we want to try our own way and implement our own ideas, He lets us go ahead with them.
We are free to discover the disastrous consequences
of going our own way. Tragically, much of Christianity today is wandering around in the wilderness of man's own good intentions and has never
been able to enter into the promised land of God's
rest where God fights our battles, where God opens
the doors, where God leads the way, where God
miraculously breaks the power of the enemy, and

where we come along behind Him and possess the land in His Name.

As we look at the world today, Organized Christianity is being thrown for loss on almost every front. We complain about the secular humanism that is running rampant in the schools of North America. We complain about the news media. We complain about Hollywood. We complain about all the sexual perversion and the abortions that are going on across this continent. We complain about the drug traffick. We complain about violence and insecurity. The list of our complaints goes on and on and on. Why should it be that the power of the enemy, the power of rebellion and the power of sin should be so strong as to displace Christianity? Why should this be? *Iniquity should not be able to displace the presence of God; the presence of God should be able to displace the darkness.*

What I believe it boils down to is that many of the people who are calling themselves God's representatives, calling themselves members of God's church, calling themselves part of the body of Christ, really, truly are not manifesting Jesus Christ through their lives, their attitudes, or their actions. They are not fighting the battle according to His plan. What many call Christianity is in reality humanism, religious humanism, and it will not, can not stand against the enemy. Religious persons and organizations are doing their own things in the name of God, expecting God to bless them, and He won't. He can't. God has some pretty powerful things to say about it. Let us read just one of them.

> *"And he cried mightily with a strong voice, saying,*
> *Babylon the great is fallen, is fallen, and is become*
> *the habitation of demons, and the hold of every un-*
> *clean spirit, and a cage of every unclean and hateful*
> *bird. For all the Gentiles have drunk of the wine of*
> *the wrath of her fornication, and the kings of the earth*
> *have committed fornication with her, and the mer-*
> *chants of the earth are waxed rich through the power*
> *of her delicacies.*
>
> *And I heard another voice from the heaven, saying,*
> *Come out of her, my people, that ye not be partakers*
> *of her sins, and that ye receive not of her plagues. For*
> *her sins have reached unto the heaven, and God has*
> *remembered her iniquities."* (Revelation 18:2-5,8)

God is talking about the fall of "Mystery Babylon". In the course of Biblical history, Babylon has symbolized many things, all the way from the ancient (Old Testament) kingdom we know as Babylon, to the early Christians calling pagan Rome, Babylon, to Babylon being a type of apostate (prostituted) Christianity which has been defiled by the man-made, economic, and political systems of the world under Satan's control. In a nutshell, the roots of Babylon are in the human selfishness which always brings mankind under bondage to the enemy. **Babylon is a type of the religious humanism that attempts to conduct the Church of God according to the ways of the world**; the world that according to the scriptures is at enmity with God. (James 4:4)

Are we going to implement God's kingdom our own way, this world's way? Or are we going to go about it God's way? The Sermon on the Mount talks about doing it God's way. So often when we receive good Bible teaching, we will say "amen" to the preacher, and leave church saying, "That message was right on." Then we go home and pigeon hole it in the Babylonian file system in our minds; we put it right in its niche, right on top of the Babylonian foundation on which we have built our lives and human organizations, and then wonder why we are not seeing God's power and glory in our lives and in our churches.

Some of you can remember back to a day when God was really moving; back when there was a real, authentic move of God, and maybe you are wondering why it isn't happening any more. In a certain sense we cannot decree when God should move, He is not our servant; we are His servants. But in another sense, if we are not where God wants us to be, and He wants to move, He will pass us by and find someone who will do it the way He wants. That's tragic. Throughout history He has passed different nations and peoples by. He dearly wanted to be received by His people, the nation of Israel. I believe the offer He gave to the Jews was a genuine offer. He wanted to bring the millennium in right then and there and begin to bless the world through the Jews, but they rejected Him, and out of the ashes of that rejection, He instituted the Christian church.

And the Christian church has a mixed record as we look back over history. There are huge sectors of the world where Christianity has made hardly any inroads. There are Muslim countries in the world today where the Christians can be numbered on the fingers of one hand. These enemy fortresses have hardly been touched by Christianity. Or worse yet, there are places where Christians have gone, only to be defeated again and again and again. But what really bothers me is that enemy power, strength and resources are growing right in the midst of what used to be Christian nations in western Europe, United States, and Canada.

The Apostle James says that when we know that which is good and don't do it, that it is sin (James 4:17). *I think one of the great sins of the Christian Church has been our failure to oppose the enemy, failure to oppose evil according to God's way and according to God's plan.*

I want to look at the Beatitudes, not just in the light of something you can define as: "Isn't this wonderful? Aren't they logical? Doesn't it all fit beautifully?", but in the light of a **battle plan**, in the light of: This is something that we can begin to practice and implement in our lives, so that we will be able to stand in the day of evil that is coming. So that when everything else is shaken, we won't be shaken. The Bible says that everything that can be shaken will be shaken (see Hebrews 12:26,27). Do you want to stand? Do you want what you believe to be your Christian faith to fall flat on its face the minute there is some adversity? Or do you want to develop Godly character in your life that will stand against any attack of the enemy, so that the storm can rage, the winds howl, and the floods rise, yet your house stands firm because it was founded on the rock. Jesus says,

> *"Therefore, whosoever hears these words of mine and does them, I will liken him unto a prudent man, who built his house upon the rock; and the rain descended, and the rivers came, and the winds blew and beat upon that house, and it did not fall, for it was founded upon a rock."* (Matthew 7:24,25)

The Greek word for house, **oíkos**, has an extended, or figurative meaning. It can mean house, or it can mean household. So Jesus was talking about a house that really represents our household or family. He was saying that if we put His teachings into practice, our families will be founded on the Rock, which is Himself, and we will not be able to be shaken, no matter what kind of storm is brewing all around us.

We are living in dangerous times. I'm coming across Christians who didn't used to believe in a literal devil or in a literal hell, and all of a sudden some of their children were almost literally sacrificed to the devil by literal Satanists. Or people who didn't believe that when the The Word of God speaks out against homosexuality and promiscuity, that it was a message for us in our present day and age. Now some of these same people are dying of AIDS, others are witnessing the death of their children or of their friends.

There are incredible forces of darkness at work today. Satan is in the business of bringing as many people down with him as he can. He realizes that his time is short. He's not playing games. Satan plays for keeps. When he louses somebody up, and that person dies that way, it's for keeps! People are really being lost, people that could even be from your own family. ***The stakes that we are playing for are incredibly important. We are talking about the priceless lives and souls of men, women and children.***

We are most definitely in a great spiritual battle for the hearts and souls of those held in bondage by the enemy. I hope and trust that the truth God has revealed to me from the Beatitudes will have as great an impact on your life and ministry as it has had on my own.

This truth was not revealed to me in an abstract manner, but through the lives of men and women of God who have had a great impact on my spiritual formation. To give due credit to all those whom God has used in my life would require that I write a separate volume, but I wish to mention a very special person that God placed in my life.

This is my father, Chad Stendal, who laid the spiritual foundation (of total commitment to the Lordship and authority of Jesus Christ) for everything that I would accomplish later in life. My dad is still my best friend, and I have called upon his God-given wisdom, insight, and discernment for help and correction throughout the writing of this manuscript.

There is a sense in which this book has been coming together for the past ten years, ever since a memorable incident that happened in early 1983. I had been in a very frustrating type of ministry since 1974, when my brother and I homesteaded a ranch in eastern Colombia with a vision to train, send out, and support Christian workers to evangelize Indian tribes. I was on a rare trip to Bogotá, the capital city of Colombia, and was lodged in the San Diego hotel downtown. It was clear to me that our ministry was in a stalemate; we were not winning over the enemy in eastern Colombia. Armed gangs of violent drug traffickers and groups of Marxist guerrillas were threatening just about every aspect of our work. But what really bothered me were the inconsistencies and defeats I was experiencing in my own personal life.

After spending some time alone in prayer in my hotel room on the seventh floor, I picked up the phone, and on an impulse called an old friend of our family. Ricardo was bubbling over with joy from a revelation he had just received from the Lord while ministering in Venezuela. In a few minutes, he met me at the San Diego and began to share it with me. The message was none other than the Beatitudes of the Sermon on the Mount! The Lord met with us in such a way that we both made a commitment to dedicate the remainder of our lives to preaching the Sermon on the Mount. Little did we know what the full ramifications of our meeting that afternoon would be.

The message of the Beatitudes turned out to be like the scroll that was given to the prophet Ezekiel (and later to the Apostle John in Revelation): it tasted sweet, but was bitter to stomach. I no sooner started preaching Jesus' message than I was put to the test (I was kidnapped for almost five months). The Lord allowed me to prove the Beatitudes (under extremely difficult circumstances) so that I could preach them with authority.

Since that time, God has opened many doors for ministry in seemingly unlikely or impossible circumstances. I have learned a great deal about God's plan for battle, as I have followed the Lord into public schools, universities, army barracks, prisons, churches, and even back into the guerrilla camps. I have learned some of God's secrets for victory and revival that I now feel great urgency to put into print.

I love a good fight. And when unjustly attacked I have learned to seek the leading and guidance of the Holy Spirit and retaliate by *Overcoming Evil With Good:* There is a huge difference between a Peacemaker and a Pacifist!

This Battle Plan, gleaned from the life and message of Jesus, has been on my heart even before I was kidnapped by terrorists in 1983 and held hostage under extreme conditions. Since then, thousands of missionaries, pastors, and Christians have been kidnapped, murdered, or forced to flee from their places of ministry in rural Colombia.

Many of those who chose to remain in the path of ever present danger have rallied around this message. A thriving Underground Church is beginning to multiply in a huge area (about the size of North Korea) in the south and east of this country where Bibles, Church Buildings, Formal Ministry, and even House Meetings have been prohibited for more than 25 years.

Severe Persecution in rural Colombia has actually served to bring real Christians together, identify the True Church, and cleanse believers from corruption so that the Promises of God can be fulfilled.

Russell M. Stendal
November, 2009

"When a man's ways please the LORD, he makes even his enemies to be at peace with him." (Proverbs 16:7)

"And they have overcome him (Satan) by the blood of the Lamb and by the word of their testimony; and they loved not their lives unto the death." (Revelation 12:11)

Chapter One

Going God's Way,
Not My Way

A LITTLE CHURCH IN A SMALL TOWN invited me as a guest speaker several years ago. Unknown to me, this congregation in western Minnesota was going through some problems. These difficulties had the potential to harm the church. The pastor, not knowing what to do, decided to bring someone in from the outside to preach in the hope that God would use an outsider (who knew nothing of their problem) to address their need. After a lot of prayer and reflection, he decided on me. The pastor got me on the phone and was overjoyed when I confirmed that I was available for the date he had in mind. He even put an ad in the local paper that I was going to be there Sunday morning and evening.

Everything was going fine until the Saturday night before I was scheduled to speak at this church.

I received a call from a dear friend who wanted to know if I could be in Winnipeg, Canada by 10:00 a.m. Monday morning to appear on a television program. Years before, at the start of my ministry, I had promised the Lord that I would not cancel a small meeting somewhere to do a larger one somewhere else. I did not want to be a respecter of persons or of churches. I understood that many times small things are more important in the Lord's work than the big things are. But now I forgot my promise to the Lord.

Sunday morning, I preached in the little church. The sermon went quite well and even though I didn't know anything about the difficulties they were having, I hit on their problem. The pastor was really excited and enthused until I told him after lunch that I needed to be in Winnipeg Monday morning by 10:00 a.m., so I wanted to get out of doing the evening service and leave right away. "No, don't do that!, he said, "Take a nap; you can sleep in my bed. Do the evening service and then drive all night if you need to."

"No, I need to be in good shape when I arrive in Winnipeg." I was thinking of being on TV and did not want to arrive with circles under my eyes. "No, I've got to go. There's this big opportunity to be effective for the Lord on television."

So I climbed in the car and started to drive (at least I thought I started to drive) to Winnipeg. I took off north on a U.S. highway and soon arrived in Montevideo, Minnesota. There is a triangular intersection there and it was raining very hard. My alternator belt started to slip, and I was getting a discharge indication because it did not want to run the lights, the blower and the wipers all at once. I found an old abandoned service station where I could drive in out of the rain and try to tighten the belt. But when I came back out on the road at this funny triangular intersection in the heavy rain, I got going the wrong way. I turned south instead of north. So, because I had to make that appointment in Winnipeg, I was driving as fast as I could go, but in the wrong direction!

After about two or three hours of driving, the discharge light came on again, so I pulled off the road and found a better place to work on the car. I pulled my blue jeans on, got out a crowbar, slid under the car, and really tightened up that alternator belt so it could not slip any more. Then I went to make a phone call. The area code on the public phone was from either the extreme south of Minnesota or the northern part of Iowa. I was chuckling to myself, "Imagine the crazy nut that brought a pay phone from Iowa and installed it all the way up here in northern Minnesota!"

I was still chuckling about that when I got back in the car and drove out to the main highway. A sign indicated north or south, so of course I pulled out north, going the right way now. I drove and drove and drove for another couple of hours. Finally I started thinking that I should have hit the interstate a long time before. Where in the world was I? I pulled over at another intersection and got out my map to find where I was.

I could find no such road in northern Minnesota, so I had to look all over the map. Finally found that I was 13 miles south of Clarkfield, which was where I had started, and I had been driving all afternoon! "Oh, no, it's almost time for the evening service!" I thought, "And I'll be driving right through Clarkfield. What if someone sees me? They'll think I was a liar when I said I had to go to Winnipeg. I better not go through the town; I better turn left at this intersection and go out to Interstate 29 and go up to Winnipeg through the Dakotas."

I turned left on the county road that intersected the US highway and drove about three or four miles, when there, before my eyes, I saw a pay phone out in the middle of a cornfield — just a cornfield and a pay phone sitting beside the road. When I saw that phone, I knew the Lord was speaking to me to pull over, so I picked up the phone, called the pastor and said, "If you still want me to speak, I'm available." The pastor was just leaving his house for the church, and I said, "I haven't got time to explain but if you still want me to share I can be there." He said, "Yes, come on down!"

So, I returned to the church and arrived quite a few minutes late. The song service was still in progress, and I wound up speaking in my greasy blue jeans. I ended up having to tell them how I had spent the afternoon. It turned out that the message was very effective and hit the nail right on the head in terms of what was wrong with some of the people. The church was reconciled and went forward in the Lord. Then I got back in the car and drove all night to Winnipeg and appeared on television the next morning. After the show, I conked out in the middle of the television studio offices, so I had to tell them what had happened too!

When our hearts are really set on serving the Lord and on doing what He wants, even if we make a mistake, and get the bit in our teeth, or become a bit confused, the Lord can still intervene and help us. I thought I was going to Winnipeg, but I had told the Lord that above and beyond anything else I wanted to serve Him and that He was in charge of my life. So, if I wanted to drive up and down the state of Minnesota that was my problem, but He was still going to securely help me arrive at the right place at the right time! As we come to be sensitive to the Lord, and as we learn to walk in His Spirit, we don't have to beat our heads against the wall so much, and it becomes easier and easier to follow Him.

God offers us complete security in Jesus Christ, if we will only submit to His authority. He is the only one who can truly overcome the enemy, and He is offering to dwell inside each and every one of us.

I'd like to briefly go over the story of Gideon (Judges Chapters 6 and 7) to put in perspective what we are going to be studying about in this book. Throughout the Bible, many times an Old Testament story contains a type or reference of Jesus Christ (in parable). King David, for instance, typified Christ in many ways. Joseph typified Jesus, Joshua also, and many others. Gideon is an outstanding example. He was the youngest son in the least important family in Israel. The angel of the Lord appeared to him and called him to lead His people to victory. Gideon checked it out; he wanted to make sure it really was the Lord. He didn't want to go following after just any spirit that was talking to him. He genuinely wanted to know if this was God, and he resolved his doubts by putting out fleeces. But once he was sure that God was really talking to him, he began to follow orders whole heartedly.

Gideon blew the trumpet and announced the message: God's people were in bondage, and they needed to overcome the enemy. You remember the story – 32,000 men answered the trumpet call to fight in the Lord's army against Midian. Then God said to Gideon, "Tell the ones who are afraid, to go home." Twenty-two thousand men went home and left Gideon with only 10,000 men to face a vastly superior enemy force.

When it comes to engaging the enemy; when it comes to standing for the Lord; when it comes to really taking on enemy strongholds; when it comes to getting the victory over sin in your own life, what is your attitude? Are you afraid to even try? Are you a person who just wants to be saved and no more? A person who just wants to do the minimum required for salvation at some vague time in the future with no desire to be saved from the habitual bondage of sin here and now?

How can we have assurance of salvation and eternal life through the power of God in the future, if we are not experiencing the power of God in our lives at present to save us and deliver us from the bondage of habitual sin here and now, through the presence of His life within us? Remember that the simplest definition of sin according to the Word of God is: **"going our own way; instead of going God's way"**.

> *"There is a way which seems right unto a man, but the end thereof are the ways of death."* (Proverbs 14:12)

> *"For the wages of sin is death, but the grace of God is eternal life in Christ Jesus our Lord."* (Romans 6:23)

> *"Jesus said unto him, I AM the way, the truth, and the life; no one comes unto the Father, but by me."* (John 14:6)

One day a dear friend of ours (a clergyman) brought a man to us who was frothing at the mouth, gritting his teeth, rolling his eyes, and screaming demonic curses. With difficulty, he got him to the door of the house, and we occupied ourselves in dealing with the situation. I turned around after a few seconds to greet our friend, wondering why he wasn't helping us, but he was gone. He got that guy to our doorstep and took off running as fast as he could go! I'm sure that is how those twenty-two thousand would-be warriors of Gideon's were. "Are you afraid?" "Yes!" "Well then, go home." And Gideon didn't have to say another word to them, they all disappeared.

That left ten thousand men, and you know how the story ends; God only chose three hundred. He asked Gideon to have them drink water and pass before him. The ones that laid down their weapons, lay down on the bank, and scooped up the water with both hands, God said were unfit for His army. But the ones who had their weapons in one hand and were ever watchful for the enemy while they lapped the water with their other hand, those were the ones He picked, the ones that really meant business. The water might typify the Holy Spirit – for our comparison, let's assume that it does.

We're talking about 10,000 Christians attempting to be filled with the provision of God's Holy Spirit, yet out of that army of 10,000; 9,700 of them were no good for facing the enemy. Why? Because they were interested in taking the water of the Holy Spirit (the power, gifts, and blessings of God) only for themselves and for filling their own needs. They were not really interested in their weapons, or aware of the enemy. They were just sitting there fat, dumb, and happy; too stupid to really understand the danger that they were in. As I travel across the country, speaking to different groups, this is the thought that has hit my mind when I have encountered churches full of people who are using the anointing and gifts that God has given them just to get things for themselves; they are not fully aware of the enemy or of the great spiritual battle raging all around us.

They are not really alert and interested in getting the job done; they're not really interested in pressing on and winning the victory. God cannot use them in His army, because if He tried to put them in the front lines of the battle, they would be wiped out. So rather than lose them, He would send them home too. Another reason He cannot use them in the battle is that when He wins the battle, they'll think they did it, and then they'll take the credit for it, and they'll become so proud that Satan will trip them up that way.

So, the 32,000 men who joined the army of God, were reduced to 300. God gave them a strange, strange plan. He told them to take 300 pitchers and 300 torches and to cover the torches with the pitchers and to take 300 hundred trumpets and to get into position inside the enemy camp in the middle of the night. Have you ever heard of such a crazy plan? It's the only plan I can think of in the Scriptures where the light is covered up. The Sermon on the Mount says we are to let our light shine and be like cities on the hill top (Matthew 5:14,15). But here the Angel of the Lord is talking about covering up the light until the proper time. If we are really going to get the victory, if we are really going to win the battle, we have to follow our orders. God has chosen to work through His people. God has chosen to use people like you and me. If God can't get us, His people, to do what He wants done when He wants it done, how is He supposed to win the battle? There's one part in the Scriptures that says He couldn't find anybody to help Him with what He was going to do, so He rolled up His sleeves and did it Himself. But it's talking about bringing terrible, terrible judgement upon the inhabitants of the earth. Do we want that? (Isaiah 63:5)

Gideon's 300 men got down into the midst of the enemy camp and broke their clay pots, exposing the light. The clay pots, I think, are a symbol of the earthen vessels that we are. God isn't really interested in polishing and smoothing and making bigger and better earthen vessels. If we are going to win the victory, the clay pots have to break in order to let His light shine out. We are still trying to keep our clay pot intact, and while at the same time we are trying to let our light shine - it's a contradiction; we can't have it both ways. If the light is to shine through us the way He wants it to, our clay pot has to break or else the light will always be hidden under the bushel.

You and I need to be willing to let Him break us of everything He does not want. We have to be willing to allow the Spirit of God to put to death the deeds of the flesh. (See Romans 8:13). Only then can God's light shine forth (through us) in a way that will totally overcome the enemy. The enemy became confused; the enemy did not know what to do. At the same time, Gideon's men blew their trumpets, which is the call of the message; that living Word of God that only He can put on our lips which will rally the people of God for battle and strike uncontrollable fear into the hearts of their enemies. The Bible says that the enemy (the Midianites) turned upon themselves, Gideon didn't even really have to kill all his enemies; they took care of most of it for him!

Then, when the Mideanites were on the run, the Bible says that the 9,700 men that were sent home, and the 22,000 men that left because they were afraid, and some guys that never showed up to be in the army in the first place, all came running out of the bushes and helped finish off the enemy and chase them out of the land. The entire nation of Israel was delivered, probably several million people. So we do not have to be a majority. It only takes a few men and women, or even children who are interested in building on the right foundation, which is the Lordship of Jesus Christ. *It takes total surrender to Him as Master and Lord, and the willingness to give up everything and follow Him; the willingness to say, "Lord, break me, make me into what You want me to be."* This is the Battle Plan.

I'm not much of a theologian, but I've told some of the theologians I know, that I believe there is only one essential doctrine that is worth fighting for. That doctrine is the **Lordship of Jesus Christ**. He's right: He's the only one that is right. It's not my opinion vs. your opinion vs. someone else's opinion, or this doctrine vs. that doctrine. *It's what does He think about it and how does He feel about it, and what does He want done about it.* That's where it's at. If we look at the Body of Christ from this perspective, He will draw all true believers together to Himself and lead them to victory (See Genesis 49:10).

The Scripture is very clear: It says, *"Unto Him (only) shall the gathering of the people be."* If we are trying to unite people under any banner other than the Lordship of Jesus Christ, we will ultimately fail, and Satan will bottle up the church again. It's not a question of whether the Protestants are better than the Catholics or the Baptists vs. the Presbyterians or the Pentecostals vs. the Charismatics. Is Jesus Christ the Lord? Is He the King? Are we willing to act on that no matter what the cost?

I have known people with their theology totally warped, with theology that would make your hair stand on end if they told it to you, but who were sold out to Jesus Christ. Jesus will work with people like this, and He'll straighten them out in the end, if they really have submitted to Him and placed their lives under His authority. Not only that, but when we give Him authority over us, He gives us security. This is how Gideon won the victory. This is how Jesus intends to win the victory over evil and purify all of the things that are wrong in our personal lives, in His church, and in the world that we live in today.

The victory is available, and in a certain sense it is free, because Jesus Christ has already won the victory. But in another sense, it will cost us everything we have, because in order to be a part of His army, to be part of Him, we have to be willing to leave everything else behind. *"For whosoever desires to save his life shall lose it, and whosoever will lose his life for my sake shall find it.* (Matthew 16:25)." This is the only way to be truly satisfied.

So, imagine that you are a "Pharisee" who has been standing there in the (spiritual) desert beside the Jordan river, listening to the preaching of John, "the Baptist". You have come under conviction from the Holy Spirit, and you have decided that you want to repent from the dead works of your organized religion, that you want to turn from going your way, from your own "good" works, and now you want to go God's way. John the Baptist has just baptized you in the Jordan river, and Jesus Christ is sitting up on the mountain; you have followed Him there, and now you are going to listen to what He has to say.

> "*And seeing the multitudes, he went up into the mountain; and when he had sat down, his disciples came unto him; and he opened his mouth and taught them, saying, ...*" (Matthew 5:1,2)

The first thing that you now have to decide is: are you one of the disciples that has left everything to follow Christ, or are you just one of the multitude that is looking on? Some of those people were probably wondering, "Boy, John the Baptist is a fiery prophet, and they say this one is even better. He does all kind of miracles. I wonder what He's going to say. He's probably going to say, 'Unless you repent, you're all going to be cast into the depths of hell and burned up.'" They were probably expecting literal fire and brimstone. And what they got was: *Blessed are the poor in spirit, for theirs is the kingdom of the heavens . . .*

A paraphrase of this verse in Aramaic, which is probably the language Jesus taught in, according to the Peshita text which is still used by the Eastern Orthodox Church, could be: *Blessed are the* **poor in pride** *for they and only they have God as their King.* The word poor here is not a word that means that you have a little bit of something, like a little bit of pride, like not too much pride. It's the word that is used for the beggar who is absolutely, totally destitute; he been completely dispossessed. The beggar who is standing there with no clothes, no food, no money, no nothing; the one who is stripped of everything.

I'm also told that in the original context there is an element of choice, so it could be translated:

***Blessed are those who choose to relinquish
their pride no matter what the cost because
they are the only ones who really have God
as their king.*** This is the only way into the Kingdom of Heaven; there is no other way. As long as
we think that we have a better idea than God, as
long as we think that we are sufficient in some way
apart from God, as long as we think that God owes
us favors, as long as we think that we can appease
God by giving Him back a little bit of what He's
given us, as long as we think that we can impose
our own will on God by worshiping Him indirectly
through intermediaries, we will not receive the full
Blessing of the Lord.

The only way to truly enter the Kingdom of God
is to recognize that we are destitute before Him and
to acknowledge that we don't have anything apart
from Him; that we need to depend on Him for everything; that we wish to bow before Him; that He
is to be sovereign over us; that we choose to have
Him dispossess us of all our pride (arrogance and
conceit).

If we could be saved by memorizing some Bible
verse, or by repeating some prayer, or even by participating in the sacraments and traditions of our
church, it would be salvation by works, not by faith.
Don't let anyone mislead you; we can only be saved
by Jesus Christ. We can only be saved by calling on
the name of the Lord Jesus Christ. By calling Him
our Lord. "Lord, I want You to be in charge. I want
to turn from going my way, I want to go Your way."
There is no in-between way. It's either our way or
His way. Either He's right, and we're wrong, or else

it's the other way around. We must turn (repent) of going our own way and place our trust (faith) in Jesus Christ, that by His grace (power) we might live a life pleasing to Him.

I've heard preachers say that repentance is no longer necessary; only believe, all we need is faith. How can we have faith without repentance? How can we go God's way if we haven't given up our own way first? Even when we talk about repentance, to many of us, for a long time myself included, it only meant repenting of the negative things that the Bible or the Church said were wrong. In other words, don't lie, don't cheat, don't murder, don't commit adultery, no fornication, no this, no that. If I had done any of these things, then they needed to be confessed and forsaken, and that is true. But this is not complete repentance. What did man take for himself? What did Adam take for himself in the Garden of Eden? How did man fall from God's grace in the first place?

God said, "You may eat the fruit of any tree in the garden, but don't eat of the fruit of the tree of the knowledge of good and evil." God said to Adam and Eve, "Don't try to decide what's right and what's wrong for yourself. Let Me decide that. And the day that you decide for yourself, by eating the fruit of the tree of the knowledge of good and evil, you will surely die." Satan said, "No, you won't die, you will be like gods, deciding good and evil." They thought that would be nice. They thought they were not going to die; that they would be enlightened. Then they partook of the fruit and died spiritually. They fell from God's grace and became mortal. And we are still fallen, and the curse is still here. The effects of the curse did not stop with Adam and Eve. **Because God had placed creation under their dominion, their fall literally signed the title deed of the earth over to Satan.**

Adam and Eve fell by appropriating the knowledge of good and evil for themselves. They fell by doing something that they thought would be good! We are preaching a repentance that is only half way. We'll let God decide what is wrong, but we'll still decide what is right. We'll pay God our tithe, but we're still going to decide what to do with the 90% that is left over. We'll go to church on Sunday, but we're still going to decide what to do with the remaining six days. We want the blessing of the Lord, but we are not willing to pay the price of returning the knowledge of good and evil back to God.

The tragic thing about this is that it is not the path to restoration; it is not the way to reobtain the blessing of God. There is a catchy word going around in Christian circles: "renewal". Exactly what is it that we are trying to renew? There are all kinds of "good" things that God doesn't want to renew. There are man-made divisions, doctrines, traditions, and barriers that we try to renew which God may want to dismantle so that his church can truly be restored.

God wants to **restore** us. Restoration is different from renewal. **Renewal can be superficial; restoration goes down as deep as it has to go to get things back on the right foundation.** The path to genuine restoration of the church requires that we be willing to dismantle some of our "good" human ideas which are really an abomination to the Lord (if they were never ordained by God in the first place), so that He can start over and complete what He originally intended (making us into men and women of integrity by conforming us to His image). Renewal can mean just polishing up our hypocrisy so that it looks nice. God does not necessarily want to renew all of the human plans, traditions, programs, and religious machinery that we have attempted to implement in His name; He wants to restore us to proper fellowship and communion with Himself. He only wants to renew those things that He deems right and that were founded on the right foundation in the first place.

The word "renew" is used less than a dozen times in scripture, the first usage being the renewal of the Kingdom of Israel under King Saul, which was a disaster (see I Samuel 11:14). In the half a dozen or so positive uses of the word "renew" in Scripture, (such as in Romans 12:2) the word is carefully qualified by the context to mean the renewal of that which sovereignly comes from God. On the other hand, the verb, "to restore" is used over one thousand times in the Word of God, and contains connotations of completion, purification, and a return to wholesomeness (peace). It is also directly related to the Hebrew greeting "shalom", which means peace (wholeness). This peace can only come from a right relationship with the Prince of Peace, not just from an absence of war.

Blessed are the poor in pride, those who choose to relinquish their pride, those who choose to have God divest them of their

pride, for they and only they have God as their King.   Do you want to have God as your King?   Do you want to belong to Him?   Do you want Him to say, "Yes, those are My people.   They belong to Me."   Or do you want Him to look at you and say, "Well, they did all kinds of wonder works, they prophesied, they even cast out demons in My name, but I never knew them.   They never did the will of my Father in heaven.   They belong to themselves.   They belong to the world and ultimately to the prince of this world. Depart from me, you workers of iniquity" (see Matthew 7:22,23) It's going to be one way or the other; there is no in-between course. Do you want to be able to stand in the presence of the Lord and look Him square in the eye and have Him say, "Well done, good and faithful servant.   You have been faithful in a few things.   Come, receive your inheritance because now I am going to put you over many things."   Do you really want this to happen?

Let us pray:

Heavenly Father, help us to understand the difference between doing things Your way and doing things our own way.   Lord, please help us to understand the importance of allowing You to be sovereign.   You have created us in Your image, and You have made us sovereign over our own little will with the ability to decide whether we are going to go Your way or whether we are going to go some other way.   That's really all our will can do.   In our own strength and our own understanding we are not capable of going Your way even when we try.   It takes Your grace; it takes Your

Spirit; it takes Your anointing; it takes You in control to be able to make us into what You want us to be; to be able to train our hands for war, so that we can stand against the enemy.

Lord, I pray that we might be willing to relinquish our good ideas, that we might be willing to relinquish the things that we consider to be rightfully ours: our time, money, talent, families, possessions, profession, whatever it may be that is holding us back from obtaining Your best. That we will become willing to return totally that which was taken from You in the garden. That You might be God not only of what is wrong, but also God of what is right. That we might be willing to say, "Lord, I have this wonderful idea, but if You don't think it's a good idea, then I'll drop it. If You've got a better idea, then I want Your best."

Lord, I don't want to wander around in the wilderness of My own good intentions. I don't want to be confined in the cage of my own mediocre ideas when Your best is spread out on a table before me; when I can dine in Your presence and go forth under Your anointing and win Your victory. Lord, may we understand the difference between the Babylonian systems of this world and Your way. May we understand that time is short, and the need is great. Fill us with Your feelings, power and anointing and raise up an army that can stand against the enemy and defeat him in Your Name, under Your leadership. Please help us to obey You down to the smallest detail and comprehend what is at stake.

Lord, as You are looking on and searching our
great nation, trying to decide what to do, whether
to let this nation reap what it has sown and go
down the drain into destruction and chaos, as has
happened to so many different countries and
peoples in the history of this world: or whether
when You look down at this nation, You see men
and women totally surrendered to Yourself who
are willing to stand in the gap and pay the price
to face the enemy in Your Name, according to
Your way, so that You can win a tremendous victory, and lift the oppression of the demonic forces,
and deliver this nation from the hands of the enemy.

Lord, that we might be found worthy in Your sight
to be called Your sons, that You might look on us
and say, "They're mine. They belong to Me. I
bought them. In spite of all their human weak-
nesses and failures, they really want Me to be in
charge. They really want to be under My authority, they really want to do things My way, so
I'm going to bless them. They're going to stand
victorious before their enemies. Their enemies
will come at them from one direction and flee in
seven directions. No weapon that is formed
against them is going to prosper. The enemy will
shoot arrows from the shadows and lie in ambush,
but I'll set My sights on the enemy and I'll shoot
My arrows at him, and he will not escape and
will not be found."

Lord, we know You can change the fate of our
country. We know that You can change our lives,
our families and our churches. Lord, may this
not be just another message, not just another book,

not just some more information we are just going
to pigeon hole and file into our Babylonian file
system, but Lord, that we might hear from You
and decide to take some risks for You; to surrender everything we have to You; to await our orders; to listen to Your still small voice; to allow
your Spirit to guide us and lead us into battle.
That the enemy might be routed right before our
very eyes.

Lord, this country needs a revival. It doesn't need
a renewal; we don't want some more of the same.
We don't want to go back to how the church was
in the '60s or however it is that we can remember
it. We don't want nostalgia. We don't want some
warm, gooey, microwaved, reheated popular reli-
giosity. Lord, we want You to make us into what
You really wanted us to be. We want to be Your
people, we want You to be able to act in and
through us. We want to be a blinding light to the
nations. We want people to be able to look at us
and have hope and want what we have so that the
non-Christians will be drawn to us like moths to a
flame, like metal filings to a magnet.

Lord, we are tired of the way we have been evan-
gelizing, we are tired of the way we have been
trying to do Your work our own way. We're tired
of taking our point, our philosophy, and our theology and trying to ram it down somebody's else's
throat. Lord, let them see You in us. Let Your
Holy Spirit of conviction fall upon the city; that
men might come from miles around with a burn-
ing desire, under intense conviction, not able to
rest until they are right with You. Oh Lord, that

we might see this happen, no matter what the personal cost.

Lord, please do whatever You have to do to us to make us into the kind of people You want us to be. We are willing to submit to Your discipline and go through Your training. Train us for battle, train us for war. Don't let Satan get away with the things he's getting away with here in our land. Prepare us to go after him, to face him, and to win ground back away from him. Lord, we are tired of retreat and defeat, we tired of seeing one Christian ministry after another bite the dust through one slip-up after another.

Lord, we know Your judgment has begun in Your own house and that You are cleaning Your temple, which is us. Please clean us up. If there is anything You need to straighten out in us, please correct it. Please make us clean. We want to wash our robes in the blood of the Lamb. We want to stand. We don't want to be Christians just to play games. We don't want to just go to meetings on Sunday morning, as if we were going to a club. Lord, we mean business. We want to seek You while You may still be found. We want to lay hold of You like Jacob did when he wrestled with you on the ground, and we don't want to let go until You bless us, no matter what it's going to cost. Jacob limped for the rest of his life, but he was blessed. Instead of being called a cheat and a conniver, you called him Israel, a Prince of God. Lord, that's what we want. We want Your blessing.

Lord, Your church is here to comfort the afflicted but You have also raised up men and women to serve You who need to afflict the comfortable. Lord, if there is something wrong in our lives, make us squirm until we set it straight. I thank You, and I praise You Lord Jesus. We worship You, Lord. We want to serve, we want to do whatever You want us to do, we want to allow You an open door to do whatever You want to do in us, we want to be available to You, we want You to use us. We want to leave here knowing that we've met with You, knowing that we've seen Your face, with a fresh anointing, with power to go forth in Your Name to take on the enemy to tear down his strongholds and to tell him that his time has come. He's not going to reign over our land any longer. We are going to challenge him.

Please, Lord Jesus, we ask you to restore that which has been destroyed, consumed by the violence, the drug traffick, selfishness, and corruption. Satan has deprived us of so many things. We want to see You light a revival that will go all over the world. We are tired of the status quo. We don't want to just go through the motions of being Christians. We want to count the cost and press on. We want to be like those 300 men of Gideon's who were willing to do battle Your way. We want to give You the credit and the glory. We are tired of seeing the hand of the enemy oppress Your people everywhere we look. Lord, speak to us, give us our orders, tell us what You want us to do. We wish to listen to You. Amen.

Training for the Battle

"Ye have said, It is vain to serve God, and what profit is it that we have kept his law and that we walk mournfully before the LORD of the hosts? We say, therefore, now, that blessed are the proud and even that those that work wickedness are prospered; those that tempted God have escaped.

Then those that feared the LORD spoke one to another, and the LORD hearkened and heard it, and a book of remembrance was written before him for those that feared the LORD and for those that think in his name.

And they shall be mine, said the LORD of the hosts, in that day when I make up my jewels; and I will spare them, as a man spares his own son that serves him. Therefore become ye converted, and ye shall make a difference between the just and the wicked, *between him that serves God and him that did not serve him.*

For, behold, the day comes that shall burn as an oven; and all the proud, and all that do wickedly shall be stubble; and the day that comes shall burn them up, said the LORD of the hosts, that it shall leave them neither root nor branch. But unto you that fear my name shall the Sun of righteousness be born, and in his wings he shall bring saving health; and ye shall go forth and jump like calves of the herd. And ye shall tread down the wicked; for they shall be ashes under the soles of your feet in the day that I make, said the LORD of the hosts.

Remember ye the law of Moses my servant, which I commanded unto him in Horeb statutes and my rights over all Israel. Behold, I send you Elijah the prophet before the coming of the great and terrible day of the LORD: and he shall convert the heart of the fathers to the sons, and the heart of the sons to the fathers, lest I come and smite the earth with destruction." (Malachi 3:14 - 4:6)

JOHN THE BAPTIST CAME AS A TYPE OF ELIJAH to prepare the way for the ministry of the Lord. In hind sight we also see that he came to herald the end of an era; the Old Testament age had ended. Most of the Jews rejected the ministry of the Lord. They turned on Him. They said, "Crucify Him! Let His blood be upon us and our children!" This is exactly what happened. The Christian Church was planted by the Holy Spirit in the ashes of the Jewish rejection of Christ, as the Gospel was then offered to the Gentiles. It is only in recent years that the nation of Israel has come back into being in the Holy Land, after almost two thousand years of blindness and continued rejection towards the Gospel of Jesus Christ (their Messiah).

The Bible says that: Jerusalem will be downtrodden by the Gentiles until the times of the Gentiles be fulfilled (See Luke 21:24). Now, with the Jews back in Jerusalem, it is clear that we are approaching the end of the age of the church. Every day that passes comes a little bit closer. We do not know exactly when, but we do know that the Lord is at the door again and we are waiting for His second coming. This is the hope that all believers have.

The prophet Malachi reported that, *We say, therefore, now, that blessed are the proud and even that those that work wickedness are prospered ...* I did a film on the cocaine traffic, and one scene showed some of the mansions that the drug traffickers are living in. There were school principals and people in the educational system who said, "Don't show that to the kids. If they see those mansions, they are going to want to live like that, and they'll all want to be drug traffickers!" We are living in a day and age when the arrogant are called blessed, when the people who can think up a way to beat the system, to traffic in drugs, to cheat, lie, or steal in order to get ahead, are looked at in many quarters with a certain amount of respect. But the Lord says that there is a day coming when He is going to act, and that the tables are going to turn.

There is a day coming which is going to be like a furnace, and all the stubble is going to be burned up. Only the gold, silver, and precious stones are going to be left. Only that which we have done in obedience to the call of Jesus Christ will have lasting, eternal value. The prophet Malachi says that for those of us who fear His (God's) name, a new day is going to dawn, a new age of righteousness. We are going to go forth on that day, and the wicked will be like ashes under our feet. *Behold, I send you Elijah the prophet before the coming of the great and terrible day of the* LORD: *and he shall convert the heart of the fathers to the sons, and the heart of the sons to the fathers, lest I come and smite the earth with destruction. (anathema, or complete destruction such as what happened to Jerusalem in A.D. 70).*

Family reconciliation is essential to God's plan. It's at the very center of God's plan for redemption. He has bought us with a great price (He gave His life for us), and his plan is to incorporate us right into His own family. We are to be a holy (righteous) nation (family) of kings and priests. There are two aspects to family reconciliation; one has to do with the family of God, and the other deals with our physical families and the need for the fathers (and here the word for father means "parent" and applies to both the father and the mother in the family) and their children's hearts to be turned towards one another. This applies to all of us. There is not one of us who is not either a father or a child. All of us either have children or we were born into a family some place. It covers all of us.

On another level, this is talking about God the Father reaching out to us and desiring us to return our hearts to Him. ***Unless we turn our hearts***

to Him, (and allow Him to change us from the inside out), we will be caught in the terrible destruction that is coming upon the whole earth at the end of this present age.

You see, that which is not pure, that which is not holy, cannot stand in the presence of the Lord. Throughout the Old Testament the people believed that if they were ever to see God they would die. Several times when the Angel of the Lord appeared to someone they said, "Woe is me, I'm going to die! I've seen God." They knew that they could not stand in the presence of God and live. That is why there was a veil between the holy place and the Holy of Holies in the Jewish temple. You could not look right into the presence of God and expect to live. But with the death of Jesus Christ that veil was rent right through the middle (see Luke 23:45). If you study Ezekiel chapters 40 through 47 you will see that in Ezekiel's temple there is no veil. The holy place and the Holy of Holies are no longer divided.

Jesus has opened the way for us to come right into the presence of God the Father. We take it lightly; we take it for granted. Many times we pray, and we say any old thing that pops into our mind. I want this; I want that; so and so bothers me. I have wondered how some of these prayers sound to the ears of God, or if God sometimes is forced to completely tune us out because we are talking utter nonsense; because our hearts are not right before Him; because we have not turned our hearts back to Him (to do what He wants).

I drove past a church the other day and saw a

sign: "Talk to God. He will listen." That sounds nice, doesn't it? But you know, there are lots of people talking to God with very little evidence that God is listening. Really, I believe a more scriptural statement would be: "We need to put all of our attention into listening to God, because He has very important things that He wants to say to us." He wants to talk to us. *We have defined prayer as us expressing ourselves to God, us talking to God: when God's definition of prayer is that He wants to communicate (two way) with us.* It's not just us telling God what to do.

Have you ever spent a couple of hours on your knees telling God how to run His universe? I have spent a lot of time telling God that He ought to do this, and He ought to do that, and that I needed this and that, giving Him a whole bunch of orders, without realizing who He is and who I am and what a great privilege that I have in being able to come before Him. I need to find out what He is trying to say to me. What does He want from me?

> *"But seek ye first the Kingdom of God and His righteousness, and all these things shall be added unto you."* (Matthew 6:33)

Several times when I have been confused in my life, not knowing the will of God, or not being able to get a clear answer on something I am asking Him about, one of the main causes that has blocked my communication with Him has been that God wanted to say something to me, and I just was not listening. He had something important He wanted to say to me, and all I wanted to do was complain about my problems and insist on trying to convince God to implement my will in these matters.

We need to look at things from God's perspective. Many times, God in His mercy reaches out to us, gives us gifts, grants us favors, and does all kinds of things for us that we do not deserve, starting with His whole plan of redemption. But as we grow and mature in the Lord, He wants to bring us to a point to where the cart and the horse are in the proper order, to where we realize who He is, to where our relationship with Him is not something we take in a superficial, frivolous manner.

What would happen if the phone rang in your house and you were told that the President was expecting you and wished to spend 15 minutes with you on such and such a day and at such and such a time? How would you treat that interview? Would you go and talk about the weather, complain about your neighbor and this and that, or would you give it some serious thought, so that you did not squander your time, so that you respected his time. So that after your interview was over, the president's impression of you would not be: "What a superficial, self-centered, selfish lout that was that just walked through my office."

I think that many times we come into the presence of God concerned only with ourselves, concerned only with things that are bothering us, not concerned with what God wants, and not concerned with the needs of those around us. This is the type of situation that the prophet Malachi is talking about. He is saying that in order to have the bless-

ing of the Lord; in order to see a day when the proud
are not called blessed; when we will again see the
distinction between the righteous and the wicked;
between those who serve God and those who do
not; then the priorities in our lives have to be in
order; we have to put God first.

In the previous chapter we dealt with the first
beatitude, the poor in spirit, the poor in pride; those
who choose to let God deal with (divest them of)
their pride. We cannot completely deal with our
own pride. Every time I start thinking that I don't
have any pride left in my life, guess what happens?
The Lord allows me to go through an experience
that reveals to me that there is still plenty of pride
left. All of us in the natural have pride. Why do we
have pride? You see, we are created in the image
of God. This means that all the qualities and at-
tributes that God has, we also have the potential to
have, but on a much smaller scale. God is sovereign over the universe, and God has allowed each
one of us to be sovereign over our little tiny will.
We can choose to serve God, or we can choose to
go our own way, which will ultimately end in bondage to Satan.

God experiences emotions; the Bible is full of
references to God's love, God's anger, God's jeal-
ousy when His people stray after someone else or
something else. God wishes to place all of these
things in their proper perspective. He wishes to
change our hearts so that His emotions can begin
to flow through us. I was reading a quote the other
night, by Oswald Chambers. He said, ***"You can-***

not think a spiritual muddle clear; you have to obey it clear"

When things are confused, when you don't know what to do, when you're not hearing the voice of the Lord clearly, it is impossible from the level of our human thinking to reason our way out of it. The only way out, the only way to regain that intimate communication with God, the only way to regain that total peace and tranquillity that comes from being in the will of God, is to begin to obey God. Take steps of obedience. This is the only way to be able to hear from God on a continual basis. If we are not willing to obey God in the small things, we will not hear Him on the big things. If we only consult Him every time there is a major decision, we'll be one of those people wandering around not knowing what the will of the Lord is and saying, "I can't hear the voice of God. I'm confused. I'm not sure if what I'm hearing is the still small voice of God or not."

God has created each and every one of us with a concience so that we can know if we are pleasing God or not. The more we obey God and respond to what we know is right, the more sensitive our concience becomes.

Now look at the next beatitude. **Blessed are those that mourn, for they shall be comforted.** The Greek word for mourn, **pénthos**, is very important. It is the term that was commonly used for mourning the dead. It can also mean a passionate grief that leads to action. Those who mourn are those who die to their own way and live to follow Christ, their master. This leads to some very hard choices. Worldly pursuits that used to provide fleeting pleasures must be renounced. Jesus tells us that, *"No man can serve two masters."* Those who truly surrender to God and submit to the authority of Christ will grieve at the status of the world around them. They will renounce ill gotten gains, as well as the pursuit of worldly power, prestige, and pleasure even if causes them great grief at the time.

Those who renounce their own way, and the ways of the world to take up their cross and follow Christ will be comforted. The Greek word, **parakaléo**, translated "comforted" has an extremely wide range of meaning. It can mean anything from calling for aid, to beseeching God in prayer, to being exhorted, encouraged (or even won over to a given plan), to comforting in times of sorrow. This is the same root as the word used in the Gospel of John for Comfortor (Holy Spirit).

When we choose to give up the ways of the world by renouncing everything that belongs to the kingdom of darkness, God responds by giving us the down payment on our inheritance in Christ: He sends us the Comfortor. The Holy Spirit will exhort and encourage us in the way of the Lord. He will convince us of the truth.

"But the Comforter, which is the Holy Spirit, whom the Father will send in my name, he shall teach you all things and bring to your remembrance, all the things that I have said unto you." (John 14:26)

"And ye shall know the truth, and the truth shall set you free." (John 8:32)

When the Holy Spirit shines God's truth into our hearts, a transformation takes place. All darkness, gloom and despair, must flee from the light of His presence. Those who are "comforted" have a heart that has been softened. It's a heart that is tender. It's a heart that operates from God's perspective and feels things the way God feels them, because it is a heart filled with His presence. It is a heart that is repentant of the sins of the past and can recognize the consequences of these mistakes. It is a heart that continues to mourn and cry out to God saying, "Lord, change me, I don't want to be like this any more", every time that the Holy Spirit brings to light something that needs to be placed on the altar and disposed of.

It is a heart that when it comes in contact with someone else who is hurting, there will be tears, and it will identify with that person. What if that were me? How would I want to be treated if it were me? What does God want me to do for this person? It's a heart that begins to feel the same way God is feeling when we come into contact with sin and with its devastation and destruction all around us. It is a heart that can begin to implement God's supreme strategy for victory; to love our enemies, to pray for those who persecute us, to overcome evil with good. It is a heart that understands the strategic importance of "turning the other cheek" and "going the extra mile".

There is another way to mourn. We can mourn

out of bitterness because we did not get our way. We've all seen what happens when a little child doesn't get his way; he pouts and stamps and begins to cry because his will has been thwarted. That kind of mourning, those kind of tears, are not blessed. It's the other way around. That's not what God is talking about here. He's talking about a heart that is set to follow Him. A heart that is there for Him to change, a hard heart that He has softened. He begins to soften our heart, when He begins to change our heart, which is what happens when genuine conversion takes place.

Once he has plowed up the hard, fallow ground, He will plant His humility, meekness, tenderness, righteousness, and mercy in our hearts. Like an expert gardener, He will continue to cultivate His good fruit, and at the same time, pull out the weeds by the roots until our hearts are pure. His goal is to form men and women of integrity, who will overcome evil with good.

Giving up our own way, and the fleeting pleasures of the world may cause us to mourn, but Jesus promises to comfort us. He will send us the Comforter: His Holy Spirit.

"Ye have heard that it was said to the ancients, Thou shalt not commit murder, and whosoever shall commit murder shall be guilty of the judgment; but I say unto you, That whosoever is angry with his brother out of control shall be in danger of the judgment, and whosoever shall insult his brother shall be in danger of the council, but whosoever shall say, Thou art impious, shall be in danger of hell.

Ye have heard that it was said to the ancients, Thou shalt not commit adultery; but I say unto you, That whosoever looks on a woman to lust after her has committed adultery with her already in his heart." (Matthew 5:21,22,27,28)

What is Jesus describing here? He is talking about someone who is no longer thinking in the legalistic terms of the law of God, but who has been softened and is repentant from the heart. To fully understand what Jesus is telling us here, we must realize that true repentance goes way beyond the letter of the law. It is not just, *Thou shalt not murder*; it's not just, *Thou shalt not commit adultery*. God's wants to deal with the very seeds and roots of rebellion (going our own way), wrong thoughts, wrong feelings in our hearts; before they ever get manifested into words and deeds.

Blessed are the meek, for they shall inherit the earth. The meek are those who submit themselves to God. **Praüs**, the Greek word translated "meek" is a very interesting word. It is the word the ancient Greeks used to describe their war horses among other things. The horse that was perfectly trained and ready for battle, that would go into battle and actually trample enemies underfoot, that would participate in the war along with the rider: this was called a meek horse. The words meek and **praüs** are not identical; the translators did the best they could, but the Greek word carries a different range of meaning from ours.

I'll tell you why the Greeks called their horses **praüs**, or meek. The reason was that when the horse got to the level of training where it would obey the master, the rider, no matter what was going on around it, so that it could be trusted in the heat of battle not to do something stupid or foolish; once the rider knew that he could trust the animal, and that it would obey him no matter what, he called it a meek horse even though it could have been a powerful, thoroughbred stallion, capable of killing enemies in the battle.

It has tremendous power, capacity, and ability; but this horse has given up its own way, and is allowing itself to be guided and ordered by the master. That is what the word **praüs** means; it means submission to the master. It doesn't mean submission to just anybody. A meek person in the Biblical sense of the word is not someone who allows just anybody to tell them what to do. It is not someone who allows everyone to trample over the top of them, and just goes with the flow. It is all of our gifts and abilities, everything that God has put into us, under His control, submitted to Him; so that even in the worst crisis imaginable, we're not going to take the bit in our teeth and bolt and go our own way. We will continue to go His way, even under intense pressure, persecution, danger, or need. This is what it means to be meek.

Look what happens to the meek: **Blessed are the meek, for they shall inherit the earth.** They will receive God's inheritance. They are the ones that are going to be placed in charge of God's creation under the Lordship of Jesus Christ; the ones who submit to Him now and allow Him to have His way in everything down to the smallest detail.

There is an interesting Scripture in the book of Job that I would like to share with you. I've seen people shy away from using Job because so much of it is the "advice" of Job's comforters. Why would all of the philosophy and doctrine of Job's comforters, who were proven wrong in the end, be included right in the Word of God? If you look over what Job's comforters said, almost all of it is true. It is very hard to disprove anything they said. Their only problem is that they misapplied the truth. It is the truth, but applied in the wrong way at the wrong time by their own human minds.

When men take God's principles and decide to apply them according to their own wisdom, it does not work. It does not provide a blessing. Job's comforters were not a blessing to Job. His crowning affliction was that he had to listen to them on top of everything else that had happened to him! But I'm not going to preach to you from words of Job's comforters. These are the words of God, out of the whirlwind from the book of Job, chapter 39.

"Hast thou given the horse strength? Hast thou clothed his neck with thunder? Canst thou make him leap as a grasshopper? The glory of his nostrils is formidable. He paws at the earth and rejoices in his strength; he goes forth to meet the armed men. He mocks fear and is not afraid; neither does he turn his face from the sword. The quiver rattles against him, the glittering spear and the shield. He swallows the ground with fierceness and rage; the sound of the shofar does not trouble him; for the blasts of the shofar fill him with courage; he smells the battle afar off, the thunder

of the princes and the sound of the battle-cry." (Job 39:19-25)

Now this is God's description of a "meek" horse. He lives listening for the call of that trumpet. It is his life to go charging into battle, submitted to the master who is on his back. This is what Jesus is talking about when He says: ***Blessed are the meek, for they shall inherit the earth.*** He's talking about people who are waiting for the sound of the trumpet blast, waiting for their orders; those who can't wait to have God send them into the middle of some terrible battle in the most unexpected place. These people have no fear because they are totally submitted to Christ. When we are totally submitted to Him, God says that perfect love casts out fear, and He is perfect love.

There is no fear (terror) when we are in Him. Let us not confuse this with another type of fear, which is the fear of the Lord – it's not a terror type of fear, it's a respect kind of fear of being afraid of displeasing Him. ***If something causes you to fear and dominates you and modifies your behavior and causes you to respond to circumstances due to your fear; if your fear is so strong that it is changing your behavior to the point where you are making decisions based on fear, I can tell you for a fact that you are not totally submitted to Jesus Christ.*** You are not operating in a meek attitude of allowing Jesus Christ to be your complete Master and Lord. There may be something that you think you have submitted to God, that maybe isn't really.

Just a few months ago, when our son was two weeks old, he got very sick and was in intensive care for five days. We were not sure what was going to happen to him. There was a little tinge of fear that went through my heart, as we were taking our baby down to the hospital. Then the thought went through my mind, "Who's baby is this? Is it mine, or is it the Lord's? Have I totally placed this child in the hands of the Lord? Am I willing for whatever God ordains for the life of this baby, my only son?" Once I double checked that, once I reaffirmed before the Lord that this was indeed the case, the fear left. Yes, it was a difficult time, and we had to run back and forth between the hospital and home, and there were all kinds of different things that needed to be done. It was tiring and exhausting, but that panic and fear were not there any more.

Fear can only get a hold of us and manipulate us and cause us to react to it when we are not totally surrendered to God. *If we are willing to do what He wants no matter what, no matter if we lose everything, no matter if they kill us, no matter if we go through all the troubles that Job went through, if that is resolved, Satan can't terrorize us with his fears any more.*

The book of Job opens with a description of the wonderful relationship that Job had with God and of all the wonderful children, property, and possessions that God had showered upon him. From Satan's perspective, Job had everything (he complained to God that the only reason Job served God was because God had put a hedge around him and had blessed him abundantly). From God's perspective, Job lacked at least one very important thing, he still needed to learn a very important lesson. This comes out in Chapter 3:

> *"For the thing which I greatly feared is come upon me and that which I was afraid of is come unto me. I never had prosperity, nor did I secure myself, neither was I at rest; yet trouble came."* (Job 3:25,26)

God's peace is not dependant on external circumstances. It is an inner state. Job had to learn to overcome his fear before he could truly become everything God wanted him to be. This is one of the reasons that God removed the hedge of protection around him, allowing Satan to strike. Even though Job was blameless in God's eyes before, during, and after his experience; God delivered him of all his fears by taking him through the middle of his worst nightmares and bringing him safely out the other side.

When I was kidnapped by the guerrillas and they threatened to kill me, the first couple of times it was, "Oh-oh, they're going to kill me!" and fear would grip me. But then in prayer before the Lord, I had to resolve: Am I willing to do and say what God wants done or said, even if they torture me, even if they shoot me? If that's the case, then they can't terrorize me any more. It takes their weapon of fear right away.

When God talks of delivering us from our fears, I believe that many times the form His deliverance takes is to bring us to the place where we are willing to go forth in His name and face our worst fears, because we are in submission to Jesus Christ, and this is all that matters. Then we become like the horse who doesn't like to stay in the stable.

He doesn't like to just be eating his corn or hay. He doesn't like to just have an easy life in the stable. He is straining his ear for the call to battle. *He mocks fear and is not afraid; neither does he turn his face from the sword. The quiver rattles against him, the glittering spear and the shield. He swallows the ground with fierceness and rage; the sound of the shofar does not trouble him; for the blasts of the shofar fill him with courage; he smells the battle afar off, the thunder of the princes and the sound of the battle-cry.* He's straining his ear, he wants to find out what the commanders are saying because he's going to follow orders. He can't wait to get into the thick of it. These are the kind of people that God wants to raise up. These are the kind of people that God wants to bless. He doesn't want us to be always living in a day when the proud are called blessed. He wants to bless His people and lead them to victory.

Meekness has to do with faith in Jesus Christ, with submitting to Jesus Christ, with obedience to Jesus Christ. Faith and obedience cannot really be separated. When James says that faith without works is dead, he's not talking about self works but of God-ordained works. In other words, if we say that we have faith in God, and we are not doing God's works, doing the work that God has called us and empowered us to do, then we are just playing games (see James 2:14-26). We won't be able to stand in a real battle, we'll be dominated by our fears;

our fears will get the better of us; Satan will be able to hem us in, and we will live our lives in a cage of fear that we, ourselves, helped him build.

I've had certain birds and little hamsters that had lived so long, for so many generations in a cage, that if you take them out of their cage, they just sit there and tremble with fear; they don't know what to do. They can't do anything. In fact, I'm told that there are animals that die when you take them out of their cage because their security is gone. Their security is the walls and the bars of their little cage, and they can't live outside of it.

Now there are other birds and animals that are so used to being free that if you put them in a cage, they will die. They can't live cooped up in cage. Which one do you want to be? Do you want to live in a cage and never see the blessing of God and never win a victory over the enemy? Do you really want to live in perpetual fear about what's going on outside those bars that you have surrounded yourself with, the fears that Satan has used to entrap you? This spirit can take many forms. It can be fear over what's going to happen to our kids; it can be fear over what could happen economically if something were to happen to our savings. Some people fear cataclysmic future events. Any area of our existence that is not totally surrendered to the Lordship of Christ is open to attack. I don't know what your area of fear is, but I do know that if you really want God to deal with it, lay yourself on the altar, and He will.

If you truly wish to submit in all areas to the

Lordship and Authority of Jesus Christ, He will train you for war so that you can win the victory over wrong desires, over fears, over the world, and over our enemy, the devil. Then it can be said of you, like the horse God describes in the book of Job: He has no fear. He's straining his ears, trying to hear the sound of the trumpet, the sound of the commanders and the battle cry. His hooves (feet) eat up the ground. He can't get to the battle fast enough when he's called upon. He wants to be right in the thick of it wherever and whenever God's moving, helping to defeat whatever stronghold of the enemy that God wants torn down. His only worry or fear, is that he continue to hear the voice of the Lord, that he not lose that intimate heart-to-heart communion with Him. "Is the Lord calling on me? Does He want me to do something? What could it possibly be?" The minute there is the slightest indication that God wants that person to move, he's gone. He takes off and goes for it like the horse that obeys even the slightest nudge from its rider.

In Matthew 5:17 Jesus says, *Think not that I am come to undo the law or the prophets ...* What was the law? The written Word of God: that is what they called the law. They called the Scriptures that they had up until then the "Law and the Prophets." It was the revealed written Word of God for them. Jesus said, "I didn't come to undo God's laws, but to fulfill them." All of the blood sacrifices; all of the ceremonial temple laws were fulfilled in Christ through His death and resurrection, and that is why we don't have to keep the symbols, types and shadows any more. Now we have the real thing.

There are many things written in the books of the Old Testament, that the Bible says are to be observed forever and ever, the Ten Commandments: all of God's principles and precepts that He has set forward as His moral law. In the New Covenant, He says He is going to write His laws on the tablets of our hearts and in our minds. He is going to imprint His law into our souls. He is going to give us the ability to think and feel the same way He thinks and feels, so that we don't have to get out a great big manual and start looking it up to see if something is right or wrong, like the Pharisees of Jesus' day. All we have to do is make sure that our hearts are totally committed to the Lord, and the Lord will be more than happy to let us feel the same way He feels about it. He will then confirm those feelings with both with His written Word and with the testimony of other Christians.

I've found myself happily doing the will of the Lord, when all of a sudden a sickening feeling will come over me, and my intimate communion with the Lord is shaken and I know that something is the matter. I can tell it right away, because there is something the matter in my heart. Something I did or said to someone else affected my intimate communion with the Lord. The best thing to do at that point is to get down on my knees and spend some time with the Lord. I need to tune out the background noise and the clutter of the things that are going on around me and allow the Lord to speak to me and put His finger on where I began to deviate from His way. I need to find out where it was that I began to grieve His Holy Spirit, and what He wants me to do in order to correct the situation.

"Think not that I am come to undo the law or the prophets; I am not come to undo, but to fulfill. For verily I say unto you, Until heaven and earth pass away, not one jot or one tittle shall pass from the law until all is fulfilled.

Whosoever therefore shall undo one of these least commandments and shall teach men so, he shall be called the least in the kingdom of the heavens; but whosoever shall do and teach them, the same shall be called great in the kingdom of the heavens. For I say unto you, That except your righteousness shall exceed the righteousness of the scribes and Pharisees, ye shall in no case enter into the kingdom of the heavens."
(Matthew 5:17-20)

The Pharisees knew many Scriptures by memory. They made great consultations about whether such and such an action was against the Scriptures, and they were very careful to follow the letter of the law. When Jesus spoke about them, He said, "Do what they say, but don't be like them." When they are talking about the Ten Commandments and these other things, that's all fine and dandy, but don't be like them. Why? Because they wanted to take their own human reasoning and understanding and use that to apply God's principles to their lives. The letter of the law put to death the spirit of the law to the point that when God Himself came to live among them, they were not able to receive Him.

Jesus walked around right in their midst, and they did not even recognize Him. The mighty works that He was doing, they said were done under the power of the Devil, that He was casting out demons under the power of the Beelzebub. Jesus said,

"And whosoever speaks a word against the Son of Man, it shall be forgiven him, but whosoever speaks against the Holy Spirit, it shall not be forgiven him, neither in this age, neither in the age to come." (Matthew 12:32)

Why? Because someone can be mistaken and may not realize who Jesus is, but when they start saying that the feats of God are not the deeds of God, that the wonders done by the Spirit of God are the doings of the devil and vice versa, there is nothing more that can be done for someone like this, because they reject God with their eyes wide open.

When we are driving down the road, there are highway signs along the way: dangerous curve ahead, slow down – workers on the way, bridge out, speed limit. As you are going down the road, you can decide for yourself. You can say, "I'm smarter than those signs. The bridge isn't really out. I know it says slow down to 35 miles per hour; but I can still go 65." When we follow this kind of reasoning, which again has to do with our pride, we take our life into our hands, and not just our own life, but the life of anyone else who might be in our car. There have been lots of terrible accidents because people did not pay attention to the signs.

As we are going along the road of life, Jesus Christ Himself, through His Holy Spirit puts warning signs along the road. He will speak to us; He will witness to us. He'll say, "Watch it! Start putting on the brakes. You're coming into a danger zone." If we still don't watch it, He'll send someone to us to tell us we are skating on thin ice. He'll warn and warn and warn. But there comes a time, if we continue to disregard all of His warnings, when we will crash.

In the Old Testament, this is what happened to His people. Moses said,

"I call the heavens and the earth to witness today against you that I have set before you life and death, blessing and cursing; therefore, choose life that both thou and thy seed may live, that thou may love the LORD thy God and that thou may hear his voice and that thou may cleave unto him; for he is thy life ..."

When they went God's way they were blessed, and when they went their own way they got into all kinds of trouble that ended with their beautiful city of Jerusalem being totally destroyed two different times. (see Deuteronomy 30:15-20)

God is the same yesterday, today and forever. But now through the death and resurrection of our Lord Jesus Christ, we can have His presence right inside of us. We (in the Church Age) have a better opportunity to live according to God's will than anyone else who has gone before us in human history. We have the opportunity to look back on all those who have gone before us and learn from their mistakes. In Colombia they have taken cars that are smashed in on all sides and set them up in some of the key intersections, so people can look and say, "See what happened to those people! We don't want that to happen to us."

Some of the greatest men of God made some horrible slip ups and lost important blessings. King

David, who was a man right after God's own heart; but because of his sin of adultery and murder, the Lord said that bloodshed would never leave his family; that he would go through all kinds of problems having to do with violence in his family from then on, even though he was personally restored. Then he went through that terrible problem with his son, Absolom. God has allowed all these examples to be recorded, so that we won't have to go through similar things; so that we can learn from what happened to other people. If we are willing to be poor in spirit and let God deal with our pride, if we are willing to mourn our own deeds and our own way God will send us the Holy Spirit that we might submit ourselves totally to Jesus Christ. If we choose His way, God says that the Kingdom of the Heavens is ours, and that we will inherit the earth.

Blessed are those who hunger and thirst for righteousness, for they shall be satisfied. The new birth, birth into the realm of the Spirit, will produce hunger and thirst for righteousness (for being filled with the character of God), just like natural babies hunger and thirst for milk. The motivation of the heart changes, and our new nature now hungers and thirsts for righteousness (for being and doing what God wants). We must feed our new nature daily by allowing the Holy Spirit to have His way in our lives. This is the requirement for continually being filled to overflowing (baptized) with the presence of God's Spirit. Those who attempt to live solely on their past experiences with God will stagnate.

We've got a situation going on now in many

churches where people are introduced to the "baptism" of the Holy Spirit by repeating funny phrases after the teacher, They are told to talk baby talk and just open their mouth and say any strange phrase that pops into their mind. That's not what it is at all. We must allow God to deal with our pride until we mourn the deeds of the old man under the old nature. It is those that mourn that will be comforted with the genuine Holy Spirit. There has to be a genuine seeking after God. We have to allow God to break the hardness of our heart. When He changes our heart and gives us His heart, it comes with that hunger and thirst for righteousness and for meekly doing things His way. ***The person who receives the genuine infilling of the presence of God does not have to strive after superficial manifestations of spirituality***; this person simply begins to bubble over, to overflow with the supernatural presence and love of God. Jesus promises a well of "living water" that will spring up out of our innermost being (John 7:38).

There are counterfeit, false spiritual experiences out there. There are many who try to bypass the only true entrance to the Kingdom of God. They refuse to enter at the narrow gate. They refuse to allow God to deal with their pride. They refuse to give up their own way. They want prosperity and blessing, but they refuse to embrace the cross of Christ. These are those who falsely think they have been saved, when they've not been saved; those who falsely think that they've been filled with the Holy Spirit, when they've not been filled with God's Spirit. They've been filled with some other spirit, some cheap spirit that came in some other way, a spirit that will neither produce nor satisfy a genuine hunger and thirst for righteousness. There are whole groups of "Christian" people who are just playing games with one another. The tragic thing when you look at them is that the fruit isn't there. The battle isn't being won. Their house is built on the sand, and when the storm comes; everything they have placed their trust in will come down with a great crash. (Matthew 7:27)

There are large sectors of Christendom where instead of a witness being given for the Lord, the overall testimony has been against the Lord. Lofty ministries have come crashing down to the ground. The end result in the eyes of the world that has been looking on has been to give the Lord a black eye. The salt has lost its savor and has been trampled underfoot (Matthew 5:13). God wants to change this. He wants to give us the victory. He wants us to be able to charge into the battle like the horse described in Job chapter 39. He doesn't want us to be bound by our fears and live in a cage that we have made for ourselves. He doesn't want Satan to be able to hem us in. He wants us to be able to go forth into victory without any fear in our hearts. God says, "He (the meek horse) laughs at fear and strains his ear for the trumpet, for the sound of the commander and the battle cry." He can't wait to engage the enemy.

"For the idols have spoken vanity and the diviners have seen a lie and have told vain dreams; they comfort in vain; therefore they went their way like sheep; they were humbled because there was no shepherd.

*My anger is kindled against the pastors, and I will visit the he goats, for the LORD of the hosts shall visit his flock, the house of Judah, and **shall make them as his horse of honour in the battle**. Out of him shall come the corner, out of him the stake, out of him the battle bow, out of him also every oppressor.*

*And they shall be as mighty men, who tread down their enemies in the mire of the streets in the battle; and they shall fight because the LORD shall be with them, **and the riders on horses shall be confounded**.*" (Zechariah 10:2-5)

In Old Testament typology, the horse represents man's effort or strength. Thus, those who do battle on horseback, trusting in horses instead of in the Lord are put to shame. On the other hand, God promises to make those who submit their gifts, abilities, and strength to Him into His own (corporate) Royal Horse, that He Himself will ride to battle and win the victory.

*"And I saw the heaven open, and behold a **white horse**; and he that was seated upon him was called Faithful and True, and in righteousness he judges and makes war."* (Revelation 19:11)

Let us pray:

Heavenly Father, we want to be Your royal horse in battle. We want to be meek before you. We want to be like Moses who was willing to listen to you, and who was patient with the people around him. He did not assert his own authority but allowed you to establish his authority as a leader, truly called by Yourself. Lord, we want to win a victory, but first of all Lord, we want to be sure our hearts are as You desire them to be.

Lord, if there is a hard spot in our hearts, we want You to break it up. We want You to come in and plough up the fallow ground. We want You to soften our hearts; to tenderize our hearts. We want You to give us Your heart. Lord, we want to feel the way that You do about the things that are wrong in our lives. We want to feel the way that You do about our gifts and our abilities and all the wonderful things that You have blessed us with. We want to be able to manage these things for You, and for this we need to have Your presence within us.

Lord, we want to go over our hearts before You. Search us, oh God, and if there be any wicked way within us, please cleanse us, Lord. Clean us up. If we are dominated by fear, please help us that we might surrender those areas to You. We ask You to conquer our fear with Your love, that we might go forward with you to the battle. That we might strain our ears for the trumpet sound, for our orders. That our thoughts and feelings might not be: Oh no, what if God asks me to do something I don't want to do? What if God were to ask me to go across the world and be a missionary in a country where I don't want to go? What if God were to ask me to give up my job or to give up my car, or my home? May we not be bound and paralyzed by fear.

Lord, that You might change our hearts so that our thoughts and our feelings might be totally different, so that we might be straining, trying to catch the sound of the commanders and the battle cry. Straining for the sound of the trumpet from afar. "Could that trumpet call be for me? Could there be a battle that God wants me to engage in some place? How can I get there? How soon can I get there?" So that we might move on to wherever the action is, to wherever the battle is, straining to hear our orders, ready to get in gear at any moment, looking to You, Lord Jesus for even the smallest things, just like the horse that has to submit to all the details and rigors of training so that it can face the real battle when it comes.

Lord, help us to look at every little detail as something important that we need to be faithful to You in, so that we might not be mediocre Christians, but that we might excel in executing whatever orders that You might give us, with whatever little tiny responsibility that You might want us to be faithful in, so that You might give us more important things as we mature. So that the day will come when we can face all of the attacks, even the most powerful attacks that the enemy can mount, so we can look the worst demon in the eye and not feel any fear but just be listening attentively for Your orders as to what do and how to put the enemy under our feet. Change our thinking, Lord, change our hearts. Let us think Your thoughts, let us feel Your feelings. Let us go forth in joy and victory to serve You. Amen

The New Covenant: God's Law Written on Our Hearts

In the last chapter we mentioned the war horse, trained for battle, snorting, stamping and straining to hear the sound of the trumpet and the shout of the commanders. This horse is described by the Greek word, **praüs**, or meek, because the horse is perfectly trained, perfectly submitted to its master, and can be relied upon to obey orders, even in the heat and confusion of battle. I would like to give you another example of meekness:

> "Now the man Moses was very meek, above all the men which were upon the face of the earth." (Numbers 12:3)

Moses started out his career by taking the law

into his own hands and killing an Egyptian. A killer, that's who Moses was, before God dealt with him out in the desert and prepared and trained him to do battle God's way. Moses submitted to God and became meek. God then used Moses even beyond the maximum potential that he could think of.

Maybe Moses stuttered; he didn't think that he could speak on God's behalf. Yet God took Moses and had him face Pharaoh, who was the most dangerous figure of the day. Pharaoh had enslaved God's people and even ordered the killing of innocent children. God sent Moses to face Pharaoh and backed him up with one of the most awesome displays of power that has ever occurred in human history. The ten plagues ended in God breaking the back of Pharaoh and his army, totally destroying them in the Red Sea, and giving freedom to His people.

If we truly submit to God and allow Him to have His way in and through us, we will see amazing events take place. God will begin to utilize us above and beyond what we consider our potential to be. Each of us has been created by God with special gifts and abilities; none of us are the same. We will never be truly happy and satisfied until we utilize our God-given gifts and abilities to their maximum potential. And we won't be able to utilize what we have to maximum potential unless we are totally surrendered to Jesus Christ; unless we are meek; unless He's the Master; unless we are submitted to Him; unless we are willing to do things His way. When God chose to interrupt the downward moral slide of human history by direct revelation of His will (law) to mankind, we should note that He chose the meekest man on earth (Moses) as a channel for His power.

I was speaking to a group of young people and I shared the experience of when I shot my foot with a .22 rifle at age fifteen. On the one hand, I had been asking the Lord to intervene in my life and help me get my schoolwork done on time. (I was studying high school by correspondence and had trouble managing my time). On the other hand, I continued to goof off and do anything except what I was supposed to be doing. As I fell further and further behind schedule (I couldn't seem to bring myself to hit the books), I continued to desperately plead with the Lord for help. I told the Lord that He could have a free hand to do anything He wanted in my life if He would only help me to get through high school on time. Finally, one evening I had a hunting accident (while I was goofing off) and shot myself in the foot. This laid me up in the hospital for quite a while (when infection set in, several doctors even suggested cutting my foot off!). I ended up developing good study habits (when I studied hard, my foot got better, and when I goofed off, it got worse). I finished my course on time, and also scored very high on my college entrance exams.

One girl came up to me after my talk and said, "I'm never going to commit my life totally to the Lord like you did. What if something like that were to happen to me!" Afterwards I thought, "What if God had not intervened in my life? What if He had not disciplined me every time that I needed it?

Where would I be today? I would be a mediocre Christian, doing mediocre things, incapable of facing the enemy, incapable of winning a victory, wandering around in the wilderness of my own good intentions, wallowing in prosperity, useless for participating in the army of God."

It was really God's mercy and God's love for me that allowed Him at several key times in my life to make me very uncomfortable, to prick the bubble of my pride, my will, and my own way, to the point where I was willing to bow to Him and say: "Okay Lord, You can have it Your way. My ideas aren't as good as I thought they were. I want Your better ideas, I want Your best way."

Without real Christians, without a living demonstration of the presence of Jesus Christ living within us, it is not possible to evangelize effectively. The Bible says that unless the Father draws men, they cannot even come to Jesus Christ (John 6:44). How is the Father going to draw them to Christ, if we represent Christ, and people look at us and cannot see Christ in us? How is this supposed to happen? (See Matthew 5:14)

God says that He wants to write His laws on the tablets of our hearts, so we will not have to be under a legalistic **law** of do's and don'ts. By His **grace** (power), He can change our hearts and motivate us from within. He wants to place His Spirit within us, and sensitize our consciences so that whenever we are in a difficult situation, we will automatically be prompted to respond in the manner that God wants.

Let's look at the Ten Commandments in Deuteronomy Chapter Five.

> *"And Moses called all Israel and said unto them, Hear, O Israel, the statutes and rights which I speak in your ears this day, that ye may learn them and keep them, to do them. The LORD our God made a covenant with us in Horeb. Not with our fathers did the LORD make this covenant, but with us, all of us who are here alive this day.*
>
> *The LORD spoke with you face to face in the mount out of the midst of the fire (I stood between the LORD and you at that time, to show you the word of the LORD, for ye were afraid by reason of the fire and did not climb the mount)...,"* (Deuteronomy 5:1-5)

Only one man went up to the mountain to receive God's law, and that man was Moses. This man has been given as an example of meekness. He was the only one who was unafraid of the fire of the presence of God. He went up the mountain while the trumpet blast and the thunder and the lightning of the presence of God caused the rest of the children of Israel to cower in fear.

When it is time to hear from God, what is our reaction? Is it fear? "No, no, no! Not me! I'm not going to have anything to do with the trumpet and with the fire and with the thunder and with the lightning! I don't want to speak face to face with God. I can't stand to listen to God. What if He were to tell me to do something that I don't want to do? What if He were to want me to give up something that I don't want to give up?" That's the way the children of Israel were. Things have not changed much with the Christian Church either. Most people would really rather be "comfortable" and have somebody else go hear from God instead; maybe their pastor, or their priest, he can go hear from God. We'll listen to him when he comes back. But we don't really want to hear from God ourselves; we don't really want to get close to that fire because it might burn something up that we hold dear. Have you ever felt like this?

So God gave Moses the Ten Commandments, literally. He wrote them with His own finger on two tablets of stone and then handed them to Moses! The Bible is the Word of God, and all Christians are more or less in agreement that it was written by inspiration of the Holy Spirit. But there is one little piece of it that was actually, literally written on tablets of stone by the fiery finger of God the Father, and that is the Ten Commandments: the moral basis of the Old Covenant. Now, God the Father, through the advent of Jesus Christ, has offered us a New Covenant; he is offering to take his blazing, fiery finger and write His laws on the tablets of our hearts and in our minds (See Jeremiah 31:33). By His grace, he wants to purify and regenerate our hearts and minds; He wants to set His Spirit within us. *The Beatitudes are to the New Covenant what the Ten Commandments are to the Old Covenant.*

Going through the Beatitudes, I hope you notice that they build on themselves. A blessing is not something that happens over night. The blessing must be planted and cultivated before it can be harvested (See Galatians 6:7). God's blessing is not something that can be institutionalized. God's blessing does not automatically reside on a nation, church, or ministry for generation after generation, regardless of what each generation has planted. There is a succession of God's blessing, but it depends on men and women in every generation who will continue to walk in the ways of the Lord. It is not possible to have a blessing of the Lord that just goes on forever unless certain conditions are met. This is a true saying: **God has sons, but He has no grandsons.**

Elisha received the double portion of the spirit (blessing) of Elijah, but there was a very important condition. He had to have his eyes on Elijah when his master was taken from Him. This meant that Elisha had to pay very close attention to the way that Elijah operated according to the Spirit of God. Elisha followed God according to the same obedience of Elijah and was blessed with a "double portion". The true Blessing and Kingdom of God will always increase (remember Jesus' parable of the mustard seed). **There are always conditions to God's promises, He never sustains his power, anointing, and blessing on those who refuse to walk according to His ways.**

Some of these conditions are found in the first three commandments. They have to do with man's relationship to God.

"I AM thy God, who brought thee out of the land of Egypt from the house of bondage. Thou shalt have no other gods before me. Thou shalt not make thee any graven image or any likeness of any thing that is

in the heavens above or that is in the earth beneath or that is in the waters beneath the earth. Thou shalt not bow down to them nor serve them, for I the LORD thy God am a jealous God, visiting the iniquity of the fathers upon the sons unto the third and fourth generation of those that hate me and showing mercy unto thousands, to those that love me and keep my commandments.

Thou shalt not take the name of the LORD thy God in vain, for the LORD will not hold him innocent that takes his name in vain. Keep the sabbath day to sanctify it, as the LORD thy God has commanded thee. Six days thou shalt labour and do all thy work, but the seventh day is the sabbath unto the LORD thy God; in it thou shalt not do any work, thou nor thy son nor thy daughter nor thy manservant nor thy maidservant nor thine ox nor thine ass nor any animal of thine nor thy stranger that is within thy gates, that thy manservant and thy maidservant may rest as well as thou. And remember that thou wast a servant in the land of Egypt and that the LORD thy God brought thee out of there with a mighty hand and by an outstretched arm; therefore, the LORD thy God has commanded thee to keep the sabbath day." (Deuteronomy 5:6-15)

Egypt is a type of our self, the flesh. It is a symbol of our human nature, and the worldly system of bondage that is produced whenever human selfishness reigns. God's plan is to deliver us from trying to do things our own way; from trying to be self-righteous in our own sight; from the bondage of "Egypt" (the flesh), which will always result in slavery to "Pharaoh" (the Devil). He has delivered us out of Egypt, out of the land of slavery to sin, the flesh, and the Devil. Now He wants to show us the path we must walk through the wilderness of trials and temptations (to purify our hearts), so that we might enter the promised land of His blessing (his Sabbath rest).

Immediately after crossing the Red Sea (symbolic of Christian baptism into the Lord Jesus Christ) the Children of Israel came to Mt. Sinai and God gave them the Law. He made a covenant (the Old Covenant) with them and inaugurated the Age of the Law. The Apostle Paul says that *the Law was our schoolmaster to bring us unto Christ* (Galatians 3:24). Now, under the New Covenant, in the Church Age, He promises to write these same laws *(... to love the Lord our God with all our heart, soul and mind; and love our nieghbor as ourself.* See Matthew 22:37,39) on the tablets of our hearts and in our minds. He promises to place His Spirit within us and give us the grace (power) to do His will.

The first commandment says: *Thou shalt have no other gods before Me.* As we look at the church, there are lots of gods that we place before the one and only God. We might not literally bow down and worship them, but any material possession that is more important to us than the Lord is an idol. When we spend more time reading the newspaper, magazines or fiction than the Word of God, there is something the matter with our priorities. We rush to look at what the secular news media wants to program into our minds, which can lead us into a mentality of fear and despair, and we do not read God's promises of what God wants to do (there are well over thirty thousand promises in the Word of God). Listen to what God wants to do: He wants to bless those who keep His commandments!

Have you ever noticed that sin feeds on itself and that evil continuously gets worse and worse? Maybe you have seen the graphs where someone put a penny out at interest 200 years ago and it turns into a trillion dollars over a certain amount of time. This is the way good and evil are. Good is always getting better while evil is continually getting worse.

Why are the sins of the fathers punished to the third and fourth generation? Have you ever seen how drug addicts and alcoholics and divorcees affect their children, and on to the grandchildren, and even on down to the great-grandchildren of the people that lived that way? In our ministry we routinely deal with cases of those who have gone through severe trauma and are emotionally scarred because their parents or grandparents turned their backs on the Lord. The Lord wants to break this.

And showing mercy unto thousands (of generations) of those that love me and keep my commandments. When we turn our back on Satan and begin to do things in the way that God wants us to do them, we can start a chain reaction of God's love that will plant godliness in our children. We can plant a blessing that will multiply and grow in our children, our children's children, and on out into infinity. This is the promise of the Lord for future generations.

Verse 11 says, *Thou shalt not take the name of*

the Lord your God in vain, for the Lord will not hold him innocent that takes his name in vain. In the Christian Church we have traditionally felt that this was swearing. But it isn't just swearing. It's saying, "Thus saith the Lord..." when the Lord did not say it. It's saying, "Hallelujah, praise the Lord," when we are not being obedient to the Lord. It's coming in and singing all the songs and saying we are in agreement with the Christian faith and identifying ourselves as the people of God, when we are really not living our life in obedience to the Lord.

Imagine a business manager of a large corporation who has control of the company check book. He is supposed to write checks to finance the needs and objectives of the company. What would happen to him if all of a sudden he started writing unauthorized company checks for a new house, a new car, a brand new swimming pool, and anything else he felt like for his own personal use? Someone like this would be put in jail in very short order. When the Lord promises that whatsoever we ask for in His name He is going to do, it is not a magical formula. Some people think that we can ask for anything we want and just tack, "in Jesus' name," on the end of our prayer, and it's supposed to happen.

When we use the name of the Lord, it means that our petition is on behalf of the Lord. In other words, what this means is that when He has called us, when He has given us our orders, and we are in His will; then when we ask according to His will, He will provide what we need to stay in His will and get His job done. This is what He is saying. We cannot take promises that apply to His will, and use them for personal gain, any more than a business manager can take the corporate funds and pocket them for whatever He pleases.

The Christian church is full of people asking for everything under the sun in Jesus' name when really it is in their own name. Some of us have a gift and anointing of persuading others of truth: the ability to be preachers, teachers, evangelists, or to minister through music. If we take our God-given gifts and start using them for our own benefit; if we take the anointing of God and pour it over our own heads; we will short circuit the blessing of the Lord, and we will be guilty of taking the name of the Lord in vain.

If we are just trying to stamp the Lord's name all over the top of our own selfish plans and ambitions (individual or corporate), to dress them up and make them look nice and acceptable: it is taking the Lord's name in vain. We may not have any literal idols, but if we are spending our time and money on "good" things that keep us from pursuing God's best, they are idols.

God wants to write His laws on the tablets of our hearts. God wants to write the essence of the Ten Commandments that the Jews could not keep in the natural, on the tablets of our hearts. He wants to change our hearts. He wants to give us His feelings. He wants to motivate us from within to hunger and thirst for His righteousness, so that He can fill and satisfy us. He wants to fill us with Himself. When we are full of the Lord and begin to get a little inkling of how God feels about sin, it has a tremendous impact on our behavior.

The first three commandments deal with our relationship with God. The next seven commandments have to do with man's relationship to man. *If our relationship with God is not right, we will not be able to maintain a satisfactory relationship with one another either.*

When we are submitted to the Lord and in a proper relationship with Him, He says, *My yoke is easy and my burden is light.* The children of Israel thought that if they went up on that mountain to hear the Word of the Lord, everything they held dear would be burned up in God's fire; they might lose their very lives; they could not come into the presence of God and live. This is what Satan will try and tell us. He will try and tell us that unless we hang onto the things that we hold dear, we won't be happy. It is not true. The only way to be happy is to die to our own selfish way and surrender everything to Jesus Christ. The happiest people I know are the ones who don't have many physical possessions, the ones that live for others and for the Lord.

> *"Honour thy father and thy mother, as the LORD thy God has commanded thee; that thy days may be prolonged and that it may go well with thee, in the land which the LORD thy God gives thee.*
>
> *Thou shalt not murder.*
>
> *Thou shalt not commit adultery.*
>
> *Thou shalt not steal.*

Thou shalt not give false testimony against thy neighbor.

Thou shalt not desire thy neighbour's wife, neither shalt thou covet thy neighbour's house, his field or his manservant or his maidservant, his ox or his ass or any thing that is thy neighbour's." (Deuteronomy 5:16-21)

In the Sermon on the Mount, Jesus takes the Ten Commandments to a new level:

"Ye have heard that it was said to the ancients, Thou shalt not commit murder, and whosoever shall commit murder shall be guilty of the judgment;"

"but I say unto you, That whosoever is angry with his brother out of control shall be in danger of the judgment, and whosoever shall insult his brother shall be in danger of the council, but whosoever shall say, Thou art impious, shall be in danger of hell." (Matthew 5:21-22)

Here Jesus applies the law to the inward state of our hearts. Hatred towards our brother is the moral equivalent of murder under the New Covenant. Lust is the same as adultery. ***Jesus tells us that the status of our hearts will determine our outward conduct.*** (Matthew 15:18-20).

Look what Moses says at the end, of the Ten Commandments:

"These words the LORD spoke unto all your congregation in the mount out of the midst of the fire, of the cloud, and of the thick darkness, with a great voice, and he added no more. And he wrote them in two

tables of stone and delivered them unto me. And it came to pass when ye heard the voice out of the midst of the darkness and saw the mountain that burned with fire that ye came near unto me, even all the princes of your tribes and your elders; and ye said, Behold, the LORD our God has shown us his glory and his greatness, and we have heard his voice out of the midst of the fire; we have seen this day that God does talk with man, and he lives.

Now, therefore, why should we die? **For this great fire will consume us; if we hear the voice of the LORD our God any more, then we shall die.**

For what is all flesh that it should hear the voice of the living God that speaks out of the midst of the fire, as we heard, and live?

Go thou near and hear all that the LORD our God shall say, and thou shalt tell us all that the LORD our God shall speak unto thee; and we will hear it, and do it." (Deuteronomy 5:22-27)

Okay, God spoke. Okay, the Bible is inspired. I believe it. But I'm going to continue to make my own plans. I'm going to continue to make up my own good ideas. Whenever the pastor has something he feels is a real revelation from God, he can share it on Sunday morning, and I'll listen. But I'm afraid of that intimate communion, that intimate contact with God, because the things that I hold dear (my own way) just might get burned up in the fire.

Let me tell you what happened to the generation that went out with this attitude after such a tremendous revelation from God. Guess what happened to them? They all died in the wilderness. None of them made it into the promised land. There had to be a new generation raised up under Joshua and Caleb that went into the promised land. The mentality of being slaves that they had brought over from Egypt, the fleshly mentality of depending on worldly comforts, the cage they brought with them, they never were able to totally escape from it. Even though God delivered them physically out of the land of Egypt with an awesome display of His power and might, He was unable to get the Egypt out of most of them and they wandered around in the wilderness until the entire generation (except two men) died.

God does not want this to happen to us. In the New Testament, it specifically says that these things are recorded so that we can learn from them (see Jude 1:5), so that they won't happen to us. God wants to speak to us. He wants His living Word to be within our hearts. He wants to have full authority over our lives. He wants to be able to discipline us when we need it. He wants to be able to bless us, to prosper us, to open and close doors for us. He wants to be able to use us effectively, but He cannot do this as long as we cling to something for ourselves instead of onto Him.

If we really want to walk a life of victory, if we really want to be used of God effectively, there is no other way but to put everything on the altar. There is no other way but to say, "Lord, there are aspects of my life that I might not even be aware of, but I want You to deal with anything that needs to be dealt with. Even if there is an area in my life where I'm not willing or capable of making the proper commitment, make me willing. You are God. You are sovereign. You can do anything."

But God has chosen to limit Himself in one little area in His relationship with man. He is a gentleman. He has manners. He is not rude or obnoxious. He does not impose Himself on people who do not want Him around. If you want your relationship with God to be aloof, He will respect your will. He won't force Himself on you. But He also says, *"Draw nigh unto Me, and I will draw nigh unto you."* and *"Blessed are the meek, for they shall inherit the earth."* They will be fulfilled and satisfied above and beyond their wildest dreams. There isn't anything that satisfies more than obeying God.

Prior to the time when I was kidnapped, I really did not have much to show for being a missionary, maybe only a handful of people that I had really influenced for God. But since that time the Lord has given me the joy of being able to work with a large number of people and has allowed me to have the satisfaction of seeing many of them grow more and more like the Lord Jesus Christ. This is real satisfaction. It is lasting satisfaction. The godly character that is developed in us or in others will be ours to enjoy for all eternity.

Blessed are those who hunger and thirst for righteousness, for they will be filled. Do you hunger and thirst for righteousness? Or is righteousness something that is optional? Is righteousness for you like dessert; you can take it or leave it? Or do you have to have it? Is it something you can't live without? Remember, righteousness means both doing what God desires and being what God designed us to be. In Spanish, Greek, and Hebrew the words for righteousness and for justice are the same word. God wants us to hunger and thirst for what is right; what He approves of, and He promises to fill us.

Don't settle for second best. Don't settle for just a superficial experience with the Lord. Don't settle just for hearing from somebody else who's heard from the Lord. Don't let anybody else get between you and God. Don't live on borrowed revelation. Don't shy away from the fire. Don't be like many in America in this day and age; they want to be filled with the Holy Spirit, they want to speak in tongues, they want to have emotional experiences, but they don't want the fire because the fire might burn something up that they hold dear. John the Baptist said:

> "I indeed baptize you in water unto repentance, but he that comes after me is mightier than I, whose shoes I am not worthy to bear; he shall baptize you in the Holy Spirit and fire, whose fan is in his hand; and he will thoroughly purge his threshing floor and gather his wheat into the storehouse, but he will burn up the chaff with fire that shall never be quenched."
> (Matthew 3:11,12)

We have taken the message of John the Baptist on repentance and cut it in half! We have decided to let God be the God of what's wrong. He can tell us what's wrong; if we have broken any of His commandments, then we will repent. But we are still going to decide what is right. We refuse to expose our "good" plans and our "good" desires to his fire, to see if there is any chaff. We are still clinging to a piece of the fruit of the tree of the knowledge of good and evil; and that half of the apple that we refuse to give up (the knowledge of choosing what is "good" for ourselves) is still blocking our access to the tree of life (the full blessing, power and glory of the risen Christ).

When it comes to the Holy Spirit, there are those who only want the "fun" things. They want the emotional experiences. They want to impress others with their spirituality. They want the "baptism" of the Holy Spirit, but they don't want the fire. So, they take half of what the Bible teaches on repentance and half of what Jesus offers us (they want His Spirit but they don't want His fire); and wonder why Satan is overcoming the Church, why we can't stand against temptation, why so much evil is going on around us, why the harvest isn't coming, why our children or our parents aren't what we think they ought to be. It is because we aren't what we ought to be. We need to return to the way the Lord Jesus Christ taught. We need to truly repent of our own way, of our good ideas, along with the things that we know to be wrong.

The Church has lost God's fire. The fire is not there like it was before. We have got to get back to the fire, we have to go back up that mountain and hear from God. We need to plunge right into the middle of all the fire and lightning that the children of Israel wanted to shy away from. "Oh, no, we don't want to hear any more from God! We don't want to be near that fire lest we die." This is what it is all about: in order to be effective for God, we have to die. We have to participate in the death and resurrection of Jesus Christ. We have to totally die to our own way; to being controlled by our corrupt natural desires. Our natural desires have to be nailed to the cross with Jesus Christ, so that the power of His resurrection life might spring forth inside of us and manifest the power of His grace to a world that is lost and dying.

This is the Gospel of the Kingdom according to Jesus Christ, not according to anybody else. This is the gospel that Jesus Christ Himself proclaimed in the Beatitudes. He taught first of all about those who are poor in spirit, the ones who have chosen to let go of their pride. Genuine repentance is the only way into the kingdom of heaven. Those who mourn with a contrite heart will be comforted. God will send the Comforter to lift them up and restore their faith. Only the genuine presence of the Holy Spirit in our lives can cause us to be meek. The meek; those who will totally submit to the Master, are the only ones who will truly inherit the earth. They are on the winning team. They will overcome the enemy.

When the Holy Spirit comes in, what does He do? He breaks the power of the flesh (circumcises our hearts) and writes the laws of God on the tablets of our hearts. We begin to respond to situations the way that God would want us to respond, in meekness and out of a restored sense of His justice, mercy, and faithfulness.

When repentance (turning from going our own way) and faith (submission to and confidence in God so that we might go His way) start producing a change in our heart, God starts giving us the desires of His heart; we start hungering and thirsting for His righteousness, because this is what God yearns for in us. He will give us that same longing, that same hunger and thirst for doing and being right. He promises to fulfill and satisfy us.

Blessed are the merciful, for they shall obtain mercy.

Mercy is more than just superficially forgiving others. **Mercy is treating other people the way we would want God to treat us if we were in the other person's shoes.** Have you ever wondered how to treat someone else? I believe that any true Christian can instinctively know how God wants us to respond to others around us no matter how difficult the situation. God says we are to love our neighbors as ourselves. What if it were me who was causing such an awful problem? How would I want to be treated? How would I want to be corrected if I needed correction? How would I want God to treat me if I were in the position of that other person? We all know how we would wish to be treated, so all we have to do is put ourselves in the other fellow's position, and God will reveal a course of action that is both just and merciful.

Mercy is not letting other people get away with

murder. ***Sometimes the most merciful thing
we can do with one of our children is some
very sharp correction.*** But unless that correction comes from a loving heart and unless a loving
relationship has been established between us and
the child, our attempt at discipline may fail because
the child will not have the proper respect for our
authority. Instead of correcting the situation, our
unmerciful application of justice will backfire and
our children will become bitter. This is why the
Bible says that the fathers are not to provoke their
children to wrath.

*"Blessed are the merciful for they shall obtain
mercy,"* really means planting mercy. It means treating other people the way that we would like to have
God treat us. The Bible says we reap what we sow.
If we are asking God for things, and we want God
to solve problems in our lives, and somebody comes
up to us with a problem we can solve, and we turn
our back on them and yet continue, "Oh Lord, please
help me," how do you think the Lord is going to
feel about us? Is He going to feel like helping us?
Is He going to feel like helping someone who is
ungrateful? Will He continue to bless someone who
partakes of His blessing and mercy and refuses to
share it with anyone else? Many times God continues to help us even when we do not deserve it, but
there is a limit to His patience.

Another aspect of this has to do with forgiveness. Humanly speaking we can forgive someone
who comes to us in repentance and says, "Oh, I'll
never do it again. Please forgive me. I'm so sorry.
I'll make it right." It is within our human capabili-

ties to say, "All right, buster, you better not do it again. I'll forgive you just this once. I won't forget it, but I'll forgive you." But what about someone who has hurt us, is continuing to hurt us, and will probably still keep on hurting us in the future? How about forgiving someone like that? In the natural, it is impossible. Jesus was the only one who could hang on the cross and say, *"Father, forgive them. They don't know what they are doing."* **If we are to truly forgive others from the heart, we need the kind of mercy that only He can place within our hearts.** If we allow Him to plant his forgiveness and mercy in our lives, they will have a cleansing, purifying effect on our hearts. But we need to remember one very important thing: Our desire to forgive others must be manifested in merciful words and deeds towards those who have wronged us in order for God's dynamic of blessing to be fulfilled in our lives and extended through us to those around us. This is how to overcome our enemies God's way.

Blessed are the pure in heart, for the they shall see God. Have you ever been confused and unable to see God? You don't know where God is, you don't know why so many difficult things are happening to you. You're confused; everything seems to be coming down around your ears. Where is God? **If you cannot see God in your life in spite of the difficult circumstances you may be going through, check your heart.** It might be that your heart is not pure before God. It might be that there is a root of bitterness, a little unforgiveness, or a lack of mercy in your heart. Even if you have been an "innocent victim" of the slights, selfishness, and abuse of those around you, you can still be emotionally scarred by what has happened if you refuse to forgive those who have hurt you. Then you will lose sight of God.

Our heart is the mirror of our soul. Our hearts are designed to reflect God. If that mirror is dirty, it will not reflect a clear image of God. Not only will we not see God, nobody else will see God reflected in us either. ***Do others see the image of Jesus Christ in you? Or is the image of Christ that they see in you a distorted image, coming out of a dirty or warped mirror that distorts a beautiful and loving God and makes Him look grotesque?*** If our hearts are pure, they will reflect God. The Bible says that we are created in the image of God. This is how we were created, and then we fell. God wants to restore His image to perfection inside each one of us by purifying our hearts. He wants us to respond to the injury and injustice in the world around us by reflecting His image. We are to overcome evil with good.

> *"Be ye therefore perfect, even as your Father who is in the heavens is perfect."* (Matthew 5:48)

With our human limitations, it is hard, if not impossible, to be perfect, so why is God asking us this of us? Because **there is one area in our lives that can be perfect and that is our heart** (our will and motivation). God wants to take our heart out, the heart of stone, and replace it with a heart of flesh, His heart; and His heart is perfect. If we want, we can have a pure heart. We can have

His heart. We can be included in the body of Jesus Christ. His heart is big enough to include all of us.

If there are others that you have excluded from your heart, others that you have kicked out of your heart, remember that it is impossible to hate your brother and love God at the same time (See 1 John 4:20). If you want Jesus to prevail in your heart, you have to open your heart to everyone. You have to be willing to have a place in your heart for your worst enemy, and the Lord will make that place because it is His heart. If you want to know how to relate to those around you, it is very simple; just have a place for them in your heart. Deal with them from the heart, and the Lord will show you what to do.

Think for a few minutes on the status of your heart. Can you see God? Or is your image of God fuzzy? Do things happen, and you say, "I have trouble getting a word from the Lord? I have trouble hearing the voice of the Lord. It's not crystal clear like it used to be, or like it ought to be." If you are not hearing the voice of the Lord clearly, there is some major surgery that needs to be done in your heart. God is not in the business of trying to polish and renew your old stone heart. He wants to do a heart transplant; He wants to give you His heart. He wants to restore His image in us. Let Him do it. Tell Him that He is free to work in your heart. Tell Him that He is free to cleanse your heart, to remove any trace of unforgiveness or bitterness.

Let us pray:

Heavenly Father, help us to repent. We can't even

really repent properly on our own. We need Your help in order to turn from our own way. We need Your help in order to see that our good ideas are not as good as we think they are. We need Your help in order to be able to submit our good ideas unto You and allow You to change them as necessary. Lord, we don't just want a superficial, emotional experience. Lord, we want the real thing. We want what John the Baptist promised. We want the Holy Spirit and fire.

Send us your fire, Lord, and take away our fear. Purge our hearts of all that is not right; circumcise our hearts so that we might please you, so that we might become the temple of your Holy Spirit. Write your commandments on the tablets of our hearts and in our minds. Show us your ways, that we might walk in them. Fill us with Your love and Your anointing so that we will have Your goals; so that we will use Your gifts properly, not just to try and obtain things for ourselves; so that we might truly build Your kingdom and edify Your body. In this day and age when much of Your house is in ruins, Lord, may we be part of Your restoration. May we be living stones in Your temple not made of hands. May we die to ourselves and live for You. Amen.

Integrity vs. Hypocrisy

I WAS SPEAKING IN A PENITENTIARY TO A GROUP OF PRIS-ONERS, and I had just finished explaining Matthew 5:21-23 about how the feelings of bitterness and anger in our hearts are equated by the Lord with murder, and how when we begin to put other people down, condemning the motives of their hearts, our relationship with them is broken. One of the inmates came up afterwards and said to me, "You're right on, brother. That was a true word. That's the way it is." I conversed with him a bit more and he said, "Yup, that's what happened to me. I started feeling anger against my brother and my father. I started insulting them and questioning their motives. Then one day I picked up a gun and shot both of them and that's why I'm here!" In a split second of bitterness, rage, and anger, he had killed his brother and his father and now he was spending his life in prison. That blew me away! I didn't know what to say. We can look on a shocking case like this with horror, but when we begin to assassinate someone's character and kick them out of our heart, God looks at it as if we had just finished murdering our brother.

The sixth beatitude is: ***Blessed are the pure in heart, for they shall see God.*** If I could sum up "the pure in heart" in one word, the word I would choose would be integrity. This is very close to the meaning of the Hebrew word "shalom" or peace which means "wholesomeness" and is derived from a root which means "to be safe". ***Integrity is the key to obtaining God's blessing;*** this is what He wants to form in us. He wants us to be men and women of integrity. Of all the verses of the Sermon on the Mount (there are 111 of them), well over half are devoted the issue of hypocrisy vs. integrity.

The greatest danger to those of us in the Christian Church after we have come into a knowledge of His saving grace is the possibility of falling into hypocrisy. You remember there was a case among the apostles of the early Church. Paul admonished Peter publicly for doing and saying things in one way privately and another way publicly. He accepted the Gentile believers privately, but when the Jews were present, he did not want to have anything to do with them.

> *"And the other Jews dissembled likewise with him, (Peter) insomuch that Barnabas also was carried away with their hypocrisy.*
>
> *But when I saw that they did not walk uprightly ac-*

cording to the truth of the gospel, I said unto Peter before them all, If thou, being a Jew, dost live after the manner of Gentiles, and not as do the Jews, why dost thou compel the Gentiles to live as do the Jews?"
(Galatians 2:13,14)

This happened right between Peter, Barnabas, and Paul. How much more danger to each and every one of us? Fortunately, for the work of the Lord in the early church, this conflict was resolved. Peter became convinced of the truth that Paul was proclaiming and not only changed his conduct, but threw his complete support behind the ministry and epistles of Paul as evidenced in Scriptures such as Acts chapter 15 and 2 Peter 3:15.

Let's look at what the Lord has to say. Hypocrisy is the exact opposite of integrity. Matthew 6 starts out like this:

"Take heed not to do your alms (acts of mercy) before men, to be seen of them; otherwise, ye have no reward of your Father who is in the heavens. Therefore, when thou doest thine alms, do not sound a trumpet before thee, as the hypocrites do in the synagogues and in the streets that they may have glory of men. Verily I say unto you, The already have their reward. But when thou doest alms, let not thy left hand know what thy right hand doeth that thine alms may be in secret; and thy Father who sees in secret, he shall reward thee openly.

And when thou prayest, thou shalt not be as the hypocrites are, for they love to pray standing in the synagogues and in the corners of the streets that they may be seen of men. Verily I say unto you, They already have their reward. But thou, when thou prayest, enter into thy chamber, and when thou hast shut thy door, pray to thy Father who is in secret; and thy Father who sees in secret shall reward thee openly.

But when ye pray, do not use vain repetitions as the worldly do, for they think that they shall be heard for their much speaking." (Matt. 6:1-8)

Then it goes on to give us what we call the Lord's prayer, which perhaps could also be called the disciples' prayer, because He wants every true disciple to pray according to these guidelines. It is a prayer exalting God and asking for God's will to be done. If we correlate the seven premises of the Lord's prayer with the beatitudes, they line up perfectly (we will look at this in Chapter Ten). If we have truly received Jesus' message (The Beatitudes) this is the response He is waiting for from our hearts:

"Ye, therefore, are to pray like this: Our Father who art in the heavens, Hallowed be thy name. Thy kingdom come. Thy will be done in earth, as it is in heaven. Give us this day our daily bread. And set us free from our debts, as we set free our debtors. And lead us not into temptation, but deliver us from evil, for thine is the kingdom and the power and the glory forever. Amen.

For if ye set men free from their trespasses, your heavenly Father will also set you free; but if ye do not set men free from their trespasses, neither will your Father set you free from your trespasses." (Matthew 6:9-15)

The Lord's Prayer is given right in the middle of

Jesus' teaching against hypocrisy. It is tragic that so many hypocrites are in the habit of repeating the "Lord's Prayer" without taking it to heart.

> *"Moreover when ye fast, do not be as the hypocrites, of a sad countenance, for they disfigure their faces that they may appear unto men to fast. Verily I say unto you. They already have their reward. But thou, when thou dost fast, anoint thine head, and wash thy face that thou appear not unto men to fast, but unto thy Father who is in secret; and thy Father, who sees in secret, shall reward thee openly."* (Matt. 6:16-18)

The Lord's pattern in the Sermon on the Mount is: don't be like that, be like this. Don't do it the way the world teaches, do it My way. Don't live according to the world's standards, live according to My standards. Be the kind of people that I want you to be.

Unfortunately for evangelical Christianity, many times the emphasis has been on believing dogma with our minds. **Undue emphasis in believing doctrinal statements (other than the written Word of God) will put a rift between us and other parts of the body of Christ if we happen to (in good faith) believe differently.** Each little group has different beliefs, and these beliefs are zealously fought over.

Not that there is anything inherently wrong with having our beliefs straight in our heads, but this is not the center. The center of Christianity is that we become the people that God wants us to be so that we can faithfully do the work that God has called us to do. Christ must dominate the very center of our being. Until we have really allowed the Lord to do a work in our hearts, it is not all that easy to get our minds straightened out. God wants to work on our hearts first. He wants to put His attitudes, His feelings, His heart within us. Then working from there, He can begin to build the logical aspects of dogma and doctrine in our minds. It was because both Paul and Peter had the same Spirit in their hearts that they were able to straighten out their doctrinal conflicts.

> *"Do not lay up for yourselves treasures upon the earth, where moth and rust corrupt, and where thieves break through and steal; but lay up for yourselves treasures in heaven, where neither moth nor rust corrupt and where thieves do not break through nor steal; for* **where your treasure is, there will your heart be also***."* (Matthew 6:19-21)

Notice that Jesus does not say where your treasure is, there your **mind** will be also. Jesus says that where your treasure is, there will your **heart** be also. The Sermon on the Mount focuses in on the attitudes of our hearts; on where our heart is. He goes on to say:

> *"The lamp of the body is the eye: if therefore thine eye is sincere, thy whole body shall be full of light. But if thine eye is evil, thy whole body shall be full of darkness. If, therefore, the light that is in thee is darkness, how great is that darkness! No one can serve two masters, for either he will hate the one and love the other or else he will hold to the one and despise the other. Ye cannot serve God and riches."* (Matthew.6:22-24)

You cannot serve both God and the things of this world. You cannot want to have a "good time" here and get all the things that the world has to offer and still be devoted to God. You have to make a decision. Either you are going to decide for what God wants; this means that you will take up your cross and follow the Lord and make sacrifices whenever He asks you to make them, or else you will go after the things of this world and lose the real treasures which are in heaven. No one can serve two masters.

One of the main problems I have seen in the Church is that there are a lot people trying to serve two masters. There is a place in the Old Testament, where God explains to the prophet Ezekiel why he destroyed His temple in Jerusalem.

> *"And he said unto me, Son of man, this is the place of my throne, and the place of the soles of my feet, in which I will dwell in the midst of the sons of Israel for ever, and my holy name, the house of Israel shall no longer defile, neither they, nor their kings, by their whoredom, nor by the carcasses of their kings in their altars.*

> *In their setting of their threshold by my threshold, and their post by my post, and a wall between me and them, they have even defiled my holy name by their abominations that they have committed; therefore I have consumed them in my anger. Now let them put away their whoredom, and the carcasses of their kings, far from me, and I will dwell in the midst of them for ever."* (Ezekiel 43:7-9)

"They place their threshold next to my threshold and their posts beside my posts . . ." In other words, where entering over the threshold was supposed to mean a decision to serve God and to be surrendered only to Him, they had established their abominations in the same place, thus giving the temple a double meaning. Some went to the temple to worship God, and others went to the same place to worship "idols." God gave them many warnings and had patience for hundreds of years, but He finally destroyed Solomon's temple because he could not co-exist with the perversion that was going on there.

After the return of a remnant of Jews from Babylon, the temple was rebuilt under Ezra and Nehemiah. Although it appears that this rebuilt temple was never the scene of the same type of idolatry that caused the destruction of Solomon's temple, by the time Christ came the moneychangers had taken over the temple. They were using God's Name and God's House just to make money. People would come from all over the world to make their offerings, and they had rules and regulations about changing money into the right currency and they made commissions on it over the offerings and sacrifices that had to be bought. There was a lot of money to be made in the temple.

Note: It was right after Jesus overthrew the moneychangers in the temple (for the second time in His ministry) that the same people who had welcomed him on Palm Sunday decided to crucify him several days later. When given the opportunity, they chose Barabbas, the robber, instead of Christ, the

Messiah. It wasn't long after this that the temple was destroyed for the second and final time.

Just before King Josiah made his reforms during what were probably the first seven years of the prophet Jeremiah's ministry, there was not even a single copy of the Scriptures (of the Law of the Lord) in the land. Then one day a priest and a scribe were counting the money in the temple and **mixed in with the money, they found the book of the law.** One of them took it to the king and said, "We found this book." King Josiah read the "book," rent his garments and said, "Great is the Lord's anger that is poured out on us because our fathers have not kept the word of the Lord; they have not acted in accordance with all that is written in this book." But apparently the scribe and the priest could not have cared less. After decades without God's written Word they finally found this "book" mixed in with the money. It had somehow become "lost" in the temple treasury (of all places). (see 2 Chronicles 34:14)

This is exactly where the Word of the Lord is in many churches and organizations today. It is mixed in with the money. The Word of the Lord is being used to make money. There are men who have made lots and lots of money by using God's name. Famous preachers who have even led many to the Lord have mixed money with the things of the Lord. It's not just the television evangelists who can be tempted in this manner. It's not just the big name preachers. It's not just the pastors of huge churches and large congregations. Each and every one of us will be tested and tried. We all have an inherent tendency toward hypocrisy, towards doing one thing in public and another thing in private.

Someone said that the true test of our character is what we do when we think no one is looking (of course God is looking all the time). If you want to find out how your kids really act and where they are in their character, observe them when they don't think you're looking. God is aware of us all the time and can constantly evaluate our character. *I think that many of us grieve His Holy Spirit continually because of things we do when we think no one is watching*.

The Sermon on the Mount goes on to talk about not worrying (Matthew 6:25-34). I think one of the primary obstacles that stops Christians from doing and being what God wants them to be is worry. This is especially true among the ladies. It seems to be a besetting sin among women to get caught up with worries and anxieties. "What if, and what if such-and such were to happen," and all kinds of thoughts like this.

When my parents were making preparations to come to Colombia as Bible translators, my mother was beset with worries all starting with what if: What if one of the children get sick? What if no one sends us any money? What if I get pregnant down there? She finally saw this as an attack of the enemy. She envisioned these thoughts as "fiery darts of the wicked one" (Ephesians 6:16), with the 'what if' like a little arrow-head at the beginning of each one. Just as she was about to give in to de-spair and quit trying to follow the Lord to the mission field, she saw that the answer was the "shield of faith". Every time one of those thoughts came, she would raise the shield of faith, saying, "The Lord will take care of it." The mental attacks soon ended. However, when we actually got to Colombia, most of the things she had worried so much about really did happen to us, and the Lord gloriously took care of us through it all!

Men have strong tendencies to sin in other areas. Men tend to be more susceptible in the area of sexual fantasies and such. Not that it is cut and dried. Men and women both can be tempted in just about any area. But with worry, fear, impure thoughts, and wrong thinking we will miss opportunity after opportunity to be effective for God. If our thoughts are not what God wants them to be, then we will not be able to speak the right word at the right time when God wants us to be able to minister to someone or deal with a problem. We will not be on the right wave length. By the time we get things figured out and get our act together, it may be too late.

Satan will try and sucker us into his traps with thoughts that may be true, but are the wrong thoughts at the wrong time; thoughts that God does not want to have dominating our minds. The Lord wants us to be thinking about doing His will, right now, today. He wants us to be thinking about what He is thinking about. When our thoughts begin to stray, it becomes a real battle for control of our minds. The Lord wants us to submit to His mind and to His thoughts. *There is a lot of extremely harmful false teaching available in the area*

of "meditation" and "mind control." Most
of these programs are very expensive and start out
trying to get the person to empty their mind and
concentrate (this can lead to interaction with and
eventual domination by evil spirits). Jesus wants
to freely fill our minds with His thoughts and ideas,
if we will accept Him.

After He is finished with the subject of worry,
Jesus continues on to that of judging others. The
first place we begin to judge others is normally in
our thoughts. We see something, we misconstrue
the evidence a little bit, we begin to make a judgment against someone else. It is very easy for this
to happen because we do not have all of the facts,
and we are never able to look into the other person's
heart. We cannot understand the other person's
motives. We are called upon by the Lord to give
the other person's motives the benefit of the doubt.
There are cases where we need to make a judgment based on "rotten fruit" or "wolves in sheep's
clothing". But when someone is our brother or sis-
ter in Christ, and the Lord has placed us into fellowship with that person, we are not to judge their
heart or condemn their motives. Any accusation
brought against a Christian leader needs to be sus-
tained by two or three witnesses (I Timothy 5:19).

I found that even in the case of those who at a
given time declared themselves my enemies, such
as the communist guerrillas or people in positions
of power who have tried to thwart our evangelistic
campaigns and ministry, I still feel it would be wrong
to judge the motives of their hearts. There is no
doubt that they are confused, and are producing

bitter fruit. In many cases there is no doubt they are our enemies. But the Lord has asked us to love our enemies and be kind to those who persecute us, to pray for them, turn the other cheek and go the extra mile. All of these proven battle tactics are written in the Sermon on the Mount.

As Christians, there is a deception that the enemy would like to place upon us. He would like to get us into one of two errors. The first would be closing off our hearts and rejecting anyone who is wrong, who has hurt us or who is causing us a problem, so that they no longer have a place in our heart. The second would be to think that maybe our enemies are really our friends, and to open up and intimately trust people whose hearts are not really right with God. Jesus says:

"Do not give that which is holy unto the dogs, neither cast ye your pearls before swine, lest they trample them under their feet and turn again and rend you."
(Matthew 7:6)

This is a severe warning. When the Jews were offering their sacrifices, one of the most sacrilegious thing that could happen would be for someone to take some sacred piece of the sacrifice and give it to one of the dogs, who would be right there after the meat. Of course pigs were an unclean animal and the Jews have always appreciated things of great value, so to give their pearls to swine was the height of squandering resources in their eyes.

Before we share intimate experiences of great value we need to be sure we are sharing them with the right people. There are intimate things that have happened in our lives, and secret things we know of in other people's lives, that can be true, but if we share them with the wrong people, we will cause more harm than good. There are certain truths that need to be kept in reserve, certain things that we may know about a man or woman that a person of integrity would not betray to someone else. ***Truth is a two edged sword that may be used to heal or to destroy.*** It keeps coming back to integrity. Integrity is the watchword. This is what God wants to develop in each one of us. He wants to form integrity in our character.

After Jesus finishes telling us not to worry about the things of this world, He says, *Take therefore no thought for the morrow, for the morrow shall take thought for the things of itself*. Right before that He said that our heavenly Father knows what we need. Then He says, *"Seek ye first the kingdom of God and His righteousness, and all these things shall be added unto you."* Again it is a question of priorities. It is so easy to get bogged down with the needs and priorities of this world.

There is something that is greatly complicating matters in our present day and age, which Jesus did not need to point out so strongly at that time (because everyone already understood the clear teaching of the Law in it's regard). The Law of the Jews and the writings of the Prophets are against lending money at usury. It was considered to be quite an abomination. They could lend money at interest to a Gentile, but not among their own people. Their own economic system was not based on interest, on banking as we know it today.

One of the principle things that causes a lot of worry about tomorrow is when we are in debt. The more the debt, the greater the worry. I know lots of people who would really like to serve God, they would like to help with God's work, but they cannot spare a cent because their monthly budget is already tied up. They have their house payment, car payment, credit card payments, loan payments and charge accounts at the major department stores. Even gas is being bought by credit card. The interest is incredible. It may soon be to the point where our entire economic system in America is going to collapse, because it is not based on reality; but instead is leveraged into place by credit. For every dollar bill that is issued by the government in the United States or Canada, the commercial banks can theoretically lend 10 or 12 times that much.

What happens if the whole thing starts to cave in and collapse? Where is that going to put the people who have their faith in money, or in the stock market, or in their savings account. They might wake up some morning, and everything they have placed their trust in could be gone. But *if our faith is in the Lord, and we invest our earthly treasures in what He wants, in His kingdom, He will always be here.* With Him, you can get a most wonderful return on your investment.

I cannot think of a better place to invest time, resources, money, or what have you, than in the Kingdom of God, seeking after His righteousness. Remember that here righteousness also means justice. It means doing and being what God thinks is right. If you spend your time worrying about how to be the kind of person that God wants you to be, and how to do the work that God wants you to do with the gifts and resources that God has given you, the Lord will supply your needs. When the world's economic system goes under, you need not go under. There might not be money to throw up on the ceiling, but the Lord will supply and will bring you through. I have had God's providence proven in my life time and time again.

One of the most difficult things for me was to get out of debt and stay out of debt. I even had some problems years ago trying to run the ministry on borrowed money. I borrowed more money than I would have borrowed just for myself, because it was for the ministry. I was going to do great things for God, and God was going to help me pay it back. Except that God did not feel this way. So when I got into debt, and the Lord did not miraculously help me to pay it back, I was really shaken. I had to work to pay it back. It took me years to get out of debt.

After that one major getting into debt, I decided the Lord did not want me to have credit cards any more, so I got rid of them and paid them off, but temptations would continue to come along. There would be something wonderful that I could do for the Lord, but I just did not have quite enough money, and there would be a way to write a postdated cheque, or to borrow some money. Every time I have ever done this, with the exception of one or two occasions where it was very clear that the Lord led me to do it and approved of it, I got myself into sticky and painful messes. The Lord was trying to teach me about not being in bondage to credit; about not selling myself into slavery; about not getting myself into a position where if He wanted to lead or guide me some other way, I would be locked in and unable to move. I have had many people come to me and say, "You know, I would like to serve the Lord full time, but I've got my house payment, this payment, that payment, and I just can't. Who would make all the payments if I were to really go out and serve God?"

I am not saying that in order to have the blessing of the Lord, we have to totally abstain from all credit, but what I am saying is that *I believe God wants to be consulted first before those of us who belong to Him get into debt.* Each debt is a form of slavery and Jesus has made it very clear that no man can serve two masters. When I promised the Lord, "Lord, I will never borrow another cent unless I ask for and obtain Your approval first," He did not authorize me to borrow another cent for the longest time. I had been addicted to credit. It was to the point where in order to pay one loan, I had to take out another one. It was like being addicted to drugs. It was terrible. Many Christians are addicted to debt, and spend the best part of their lives feeding banks, insurance companies, and finance companies because the interest adds up and up and up. These companies are making a killing off of God's people.

The Word of the Lord is very clear. It says that if we follow Him and obey His

commands and do what He tells us to do, then we will not be the ones borrowing money, we will be the ones who are lending money to those who do not know Him. He wants us to be the head and not the tail. God has not declared a law against borrowing and lending (*He says, "Give to him who asks of you and do not turn away from the one who wants to borrow from you"*); but He wants it in the proper order. He want us to be the ones who have the resources, because we have His Blessing, so that we can be the ones who are lending to other people who are in need. He wants them to be subservient to us; not us subservient to them.

In the Bible, God makes it very clear that the borrower is the servant of the lender; really the slave of the lender (Proverbs 22:7). Today we do not believe in slavery, but many people still live in slavery. They have sold themselves into financial slavery, into economic bondage. This is a very sad way to live as a Christian. If you are in the position of worrying about your finances; worrying about not having enough for this or that; worrying how to make your next credit card payment, I would suggest you go over every detail of your finances before the Lord, and make a commitment to Him that you are not going to borrow or spend another cent unless He approves; that you are going to consult Him prior to each and every financial transaction you make. If there are credit cards or debts that are bogging you down and holding you back from being free in the Lord to trust Him without worry and fear, then you want to start paying these things off and getting rid of them. You want Him to help you get to a position where if there are any debts, it is because you have been doing the lending, not the borrowing!

The Lord wants to turn this thing around. I believe that if we truly obey God in regard to our finances, that when the economic collapse comes, if we are where God wants us to be; then we will be the ones who will be reaping the benefits when everyone else is going under. Resources will be falling into our hands instead of us being the ones that are losing everything in the crash.

If you study the great economic crashes of the past, many lost everything, but there were certain people who wound up with everyone else's wealth in their hands, because when everything became cheap, the ones who had the resources; the ones who were solvent, went out and bought it all up. There were tremendous fortunes made at the same time that lots of people lost their shirts. The ones who were heavily leveraged into debt never came out. They were the ones jumping off of buildings and committing suicide.

We need to make sure that we are where God wants us to be. I do not think that this is a message that we are to store up goods or horde or anything like that. I have not felt happy hearing "Christian" fear mongers say that we should bury gold under our refrigerators or hoard up seven years of provisions, so that we can make it through the tribulation. What God wants is for us to handle our resources and finances according to His will. He wants to be in charge. He wants to use us to help meet the needs of others around us. If we start hanging on to things, it bottlenecks God's economy.

When we are free with our resources, not to the point of getting into debt, but saying, "Here I am, Lord, and what I have is Yours. How do You want it used?" Then we can live without fear of tomorrow, and the Lord can begin to bless. He can bless others through us, and others can see God in us. They can feel His hand. Then He can truly prosper and protect us. How are we to overcome evil with good, if we selfishly hoard our resources? God doesn't want His people to retreat, or even to circle their wagons. He wants to lead them to battle and win the victory.

So what are we to pray for when we pray? *One of the things we are supposed to do when we pray is listen to the Lord.* This is something that many "Christians" do not do. We are told not to pray like the pagans who think that they will be heard because of their many words. When we pray, God wants to talk to us. We can express ourselves to Him, and share what is on our hearts and minds, but we need to listen to the Lord. We need to begin our prayer with "Our Father, Who art in heaven." Not a singular personal pronoun, but a collective pronoun. *Our* Father. *We should be as concerned about the needs of those around us as we are about our own needs. God is not pleased with the selfish prayers that many of us pray.*

If your children were to come to you, continually asking for things for themselves, always for something more, you would get a bit tired of it. But what if your child was always concerned about those around him (or her), and every time he came with a petition it was for some other needy kid? What would your concept be of your child? Would it touch your heart as well and would you be interested in helping your child help those around them? This should definitely be something you would want to implement in your child's life. This is the way I think that God feels when we come to Him with the needs of those around us, putting the needs of others first.

> *"Ask, and it shall be given you; seek, and ye shall find; knock, and it shall be opened unto you; for every one that asks receives, and he that seeks finds, and to him that knocks it shall be opened."* (Matthew 7:7-8)

The Greek verb in the original language denotes continuous action that is an attribute of the person. We do not have that tense in English, but it would be like saying, "For everyone who is an asker, receives; everyone who is a seeker, finds; to everyone who is a knocker, the door will be opened." There is a quality of perseverance, but not perseverance after the things of the world. Jesus is talking about asking, seeking and knocking for (setting our sights on) the real wealth and riches that God has to offer: wisdom, understanding, discernment, the fruit of the Holy Spirit, and for His gifts. All the valuable things that He really wants to endow upon us are available only to those who persistently set their hearts to follow Him and go after His best.

God will not cast His pearls before "swine." He will not throw what is sacred to the "dogs." He will not share His wisdom, understanding and intimate secrets of The Kingdom with those who are unworthy. He will not throw precious pearls of truth out there for anyone who superficially wants to know about them. If you really want to be used of God, it will take persistence on your part: asking, seeking, and knocking.

> *"Or what man is there of you, whom, if his son aks for bread, will he give him a stone? Or if he asks for fish, will he give him a serpent? If ye then, being evil, know how to give good gifts unto your children, how much more shall your Father who is in the heavens give good things to those that ask him?*
>
> *Therefore, all things whatsoever ye desire that men should do unto you, so also shall ye do unto them, for this is the law and the prophets."* (Matthew 7:9-12)

Again, it comes back to righteousness (being and doing what God wants), in our relationship with those around us, in the same manner that we would want others to do unto us. We can always know how God would want us to treat someone else, because we can always put ourselves in that person's position and know how we ourselves would want to be treated under the same circumstances.

Many of those calling themselves Christians do not really seek what is righteous. They make a case for going their own way, and because they still feel a little guilt in their conscience; then to get another stamp of approval, or to get out from under responsibility, they come in for counselling. They will seek the pastor or counsellor and seek to reenforce the humanistic rationale that they have made up for themselves.

It is amazing to see the number of men who come in for family counselling because their wife needs to be straightened out; or if it's the wife, then the husband needs to be straightened out; or if it's the parents, then the children need straightening out. They are always looking for someone else to straighten out their loved one. The crusades we used to have in Colombia focused on the area of family reconciliation. Everyone has family problems. Everyone has someone in their family they feel needs to be straightened out. So if we advertised that in our meetings there would be lots of good advise on the family, people would come in, maybe not so much because they thought they needed anything, but because they had this poor soul in their family that they had to get straightened out!

God looks at things from a different perspective. He says in verse 13,

> *"Enter ye in at the narrow gate, for the way that leads to destruction is wide and spacious, and those who follow it are many; because narrow is the gate, and confined is the way which leads unto life, and there are few that find it."* (Matthew 7:13,14)

God is interested in each and every one of us. He is interested in getting our priorities right, and that we become men and women of integrity. Precisely when we think we are okay, when we think we have arrived, when we think we are the sole owners of the truth; that is when we are in the most danger of falling into hypocrisy. This is what happened to the Jews, and what has happened repeatedly throughout the history of organized Christianity. Hypocrisy in its final forms actually begins to take the credit for what God is doing.

The history of Christian church is full of many sad examples of those in leadership who have taken the credit for what God has done and in so doing they have short circuited the power of God and plunged the church into black darkness for long periods of time. Right now, even in the age in which we are living, the church is not in very good shape. It is asleep. There are very few people with sharp discernment, who are totally sold out to the Lordship and authority of Jesus Christ. There are not too many men or women of integrity who will preach the true word of the Lord without mixing money up into the deal.

The prophet Daniel said that there would come a time when the abomination of desolation would be set up right in the Holy Place, and that is exactly what happened preceding the destruction of Jerusalem in 70 A.D. as money changers and merchants continued to dominate the temple. Finally, according to the Jewish historian, Josephus, there was a terrible battle between two factions of Jews fought right within the temple citadel over control of the vast stores of food as well as the treasure. The Sanctuary was profaned with the bloody slaughter of Jews by Jews (see Daniel 11:31 and Matthew 24:15). This was the signal to the Church to flee to the mountains, and they were not caught up in the Roman destruction of Jerusalem.

Many of these physical lessons of the past also have a spiritual fulfillment. There is still an abomination in the Holy Place. There are a lot of "Christian" people / groups / denominations who have placed their thresholds beside God's, and you get in to their "church", not by surrendering to the Lordship of Jesus Christ, like it says in the Word of God, but by agreeing to their doctrine and by participating in their religious rituals. The person who is not submitted to the Lordship of Jesus Christ can many times open themselves up to be used by a false spirit instead of by the Holy Spirit. There are many abominations that are being done today in the name of the Lord by people who are hypocrites; who say one thing and do another.

Some of the biggest names in evangelism have bit the dust recently because of this problem, because their private lives were one thing, and their public ministry was another, and the two were entirely different, not in agreement, not in correlation. There was such an abomination going on, that when it finally came to light, it brought their entire ministry down.

We do not want that to happen to us. We want to enter in at the narrow gate. The narrow gate is so tight that we cannot take anything with us. We can just barely go through with nothing else. There is no room for our pride to go through with us, or for our material possessiones or for anything else that we would want to clutch onto. There is just room for us, stripped of everything, being willing to submit ourselves to God and to do what He wants. This is the narrow gate, the road to life, and Jesus says that few find it.

> *"Enter ye in at the narrow gate, for the way that leads to destruction is wide and spacious, and those who follow it are many; because narrow is the gate, and confined is the way which leads unto life, and there are few that find it."* (Matthew 7:13,14)

What are we going to do? Is our goal going to be integrity? If it is, if we want God to continue purifying our hearts, if we are really after His blessing above and beyond anything else, if we truly want to be peacemakers, then the last two Beatitudes say:

> *"Blessed are those who suffer persecution for righteousness' sake, for theirs is the kingdom of the heavens. Blessed are ye when men shall revile you and persecute you and shall say all manner of evil against you falsely for my sake. Rejoice and be exceeding glad, for great is your reward in the heavens; for so they persecuted the prophets who were before you."* (Matthew 5:10-12)

Friends, if everyone, all the time, always speaks well of you, it could be a bad sign; because that is what happens to hypocrites. Let's ask the Lord to deliver us from a spirit of hypocrisy and to send us His fire to burn up everything that is not good, so that we will be men and women of integrity and able to stand through the time of shaking and judgment that I am convinced is coming upon the church. God says that the wood, hay and stubble will be burned up on the day that He acts, and only the gold, silver and precious stones will be left.

Let us pray:

Heavenly Father, I pray that we would be as gold, silver, and precious stones, purified in the fire, for You use to build Your true Kingdom; that we would allow You, Lord, to give us Your real treasures that cannot be destroyed; that we would be men and women of integrity; that those around us would be able to see You in us. We know that those who are full of hypocrisy may become vicious when they come in contact with someone full of Your integrity. They cannot stand it, because it reveals them for what they are. But Lord, if we are persecuted, let it be because of You, because we have stood for being what You want us to be and for doing what You want us to do.

Please Lord, do not allow us to be persecuted just because of our own stupidity, because we needlessly offended someone else by taking Your truth and using it in the wrong way; if instead of using it to heal, we have used it to hurt someone else. Help us Lord, to understand Your priorities, to be persistent in asking, seeking and knocking; but for the real treasures, the ones that last forever.

Help us to enter the narrow gate and not get stuck in the doorway, but to get through it and to become divested of everything that would hold us back, so that we can come out into Your blessing, into Your joy, into Your rest. So that what we are doing will stand like the house built on the rock.

So that no matter how intense the storm or how severe the flood or how strong the wind blows and beats upon our house, that what we are doing will stand, because it is part of what you are building. Amen.

Chapter Five

The Peacemakers: Those Whom God Identifies as His Sons

*BLESSED ARE THE PEACEMAKERS, **for they shall be called the sons of God**.* This is the focal point of the Beatitudes. It has to do with the purpose of Jesus' ministry here on this earth. One of His main objectives in coming here is that we might be called the sons of God. Notice it does not say Blessed are the peacemakers, for they shall call themselves the sons of God. It says, Blessed are the peacemakers, for they shall be called the sons of God. Like when the word, "Christian", was first used to describe the followers of Christ in Antioch, because they were like Him.

If the Beatitudes have truly been planted in our hearts, and if we have honestly set our will to follow God; then as He begins to work in and through us, it will become readily apparent to those around us, that we are indeed the sons of God. Sons, in this usage, in the original language, has no gender. This beatitude also directly implies that God will call us His sons.

In the Christian world that we live in today (even in the non-Christian world of other religions), there are many people who call themselves sons of God. In a certain context there have been times in the past when even Satan was included in this. In the book of Job it says that the sons of God were gathered and Satan was among them (see Job 1:6). In other words, there have been times when it has been convenient even for Satan to identify himself as a son of God. The fact that someone identifies themselves as a son of God is not the important thing. The important thing is what we are in God's eyes. Who are the ones that He identifies as His sons?

"Keep yourselves also from the false prophets, who come to you in sheep's clothing, but inwardly they are ravening wolves. Ye shall know them by their fruits. Do men gather grapes of thorns, or figs of thistles? Even so every good tree brings forth good fruit, but a corrupt tree brings forth evil fruit. A good tree cannot bring forth evil fruit, neither can a corrupt tree bring forth good fruit." (Matthew 7:15-18)

There is a bit of confusion on the last phrase of this Scripture due to difficulties invlolved in translating it into the English language. I have gone over this passage word by word and phrase by phrase. What this Scripture means to me is that a good tree is a healthy tree. A corrupt tree is a rotten tree. You can have two trees of the same species - two apple trees, two cherry trees – but one of them is rotten to the core and the other is sound and healthy. What the Lord is saying is that likewise to the obvious fact that you cannot get grapes from thornbushes or figs from thistles, you cannot get good healthy fruit out of a rotten fruit tree. A rotten apple tree will produce scraggly, rotten, little apples. A good or healthy tree will produce wholesome, delicious fruit. The old man has his roots (nature) in Adam. The new man is firmly rooted in Christ.

I have a friend in Canada who races sled dogs. I commented on how friendly his dogs were, in comparison to other people's sled dogs I had seen that seemed vicious. Then he told me his secret. At an early age (around 28 days I believe), the dogs imprint psychologically. If the puppies are around friendly people at that time, they will imprint on them and be friendly for the rest of their lives towards humans. If they are around a mother dog who is aloof, withdrawn, and distrustful, then that is the way they become. So, at the critical time, my friend takes all the pups into his cabin and has his kids play with them. To my knowledge he has never had a mean dog yet. This principle is also very important in Christianity. Jesus wants us to imprint on Himself. He also wants those whom we would lead to the Lord to imprint on Himself as He is reflected through each one of our lives.

As I have travelled around speaking to many different groups I have observed that, just like those sled dogs, new Christians tend to imprint on the leadership of the group in which they came into the new birth. For example, if you have a proud, haughty leader, that same trait seems to run rampant through the group of people who are being discipled under that man's ministry. When we are reaching out to others and having an effect on their lives, they will imprint on us to a certain extent. If we are a rotten tree, all we will be able to produce will be scraggly little rotten apples. The ones we are leading to the Lord and trying to disciple could wind up just like us.

The Lord says right in the first chapter of Genesis that He created the world so that every living thing (plant or animal) reproduces after its own kind. If you have a church where the leadership is superficial and carnal, that church will reproduce superficial carnal Christians who will not be able to stand in the day of battle, the day of evil. On the other hand, if there is Godly character, if there is true submission to the authority and Lordship of Jesus Christ, if people can truly see Jesus Christ in us, they will imprint on Him.

I have caught a number of parrots in the jungle over the years, and these birds have the capability of learning to talk. They cannot talk like you and I, but some of the better ones can pick up a vocabulary of 30 or more words. I have even seen cases where parrots could use those words in a seemingly intelligent fashion. But the parrot does not necessarily pick up the words you want to teach it. It is prone to picking up words at certain key times. If the bird is out in the rain and gets soaked, it likes to talk when it is wet. It will sit and talk its head off and pick up on all sorts of phrases when it is cold, wet and shivering.

You can sit with a dry parrot and try to teach it all you want, but it has to be out in the rain to understand. It is under situations of seeming adversity that these birds pick up whatever they are going to repeat for the rest of their lives. You can have all your set phrases that you are trying to teach the parrot and spend time continuously repeating them, and then at the wrong moment, you can make one slip of the tongue, and that is what you will listen to for the rest of the life of that parrot. It will even catch the exact tone of your voice. All you have to do is say one angry word to your wife or to your child, or one swear word, and that is probably what will be repeated. You have to get rid of the parrot, if you do not want to listen to that phrase.

> *"Every tree that does not bring forth good fruit is hewn down and cast into the fire. So that by their fruits ye shall know them."* (Matthew 7:19,20)

One tree produces little, scraggly, wormy, rotten apples and the other produces great big delicious, luscious apples. Same species, but one is rotten to the core. We are talking about human beings who are created in the image of God. Some of them allow themselves to be molded and imprinted on the character of God through a total change of heart. Others pretend to do this but their heart stays the same. Out of our heart springs what flows out of our mouths (Mt. 15:18). A spring cannot have two kinds of water. It cannot be both salty and sweet at the same time.

> *"Not every one that saith unto me, Lord, Lord, shall enter into the Kingdom of the heavens, but he that doeth the will of my Father who is in the heavens. Many will say to me in that day, Lord, Lord, have we not prophesied in thy name? and in thy name have cast out devils? and in thy name done many wonderful works? And then I will profess unto them, I never knew you; depart from me, ye that work iniquity."* (Matthew 7:21-23)

Have you ever taken a bite into a piece of fruit and discovered it was rotten, and that it tasted terrible, or there was a worm in it, and you had to spit it out? It nauseated you, and you could not stand to eat it. This is what God is talking about here. He is talking about getting hold of some rotten fruit that He just could not stand to eat.

Blessed are the peacemakers, for they shall be called the sons of God. The word peacemaker is an interesting term. Another way of saying it would be, the ones who put together or build peace. The ones who reflect peace. We don't really make our own peace, because our peace comes from God, but the peacemakers are the ones who radiate or project God's peace around them wherever they go.

One day during the time I was held hostage by communist guerrillas, I had been talking to their nurse. All of a sudden there were tears in her eyes. She looked at me and said, "I envy you because you have your own personal peace, and I don't." She was the one with the machine gun and the hand grenade; the physical weapons, and I was the one tied up while she was pointing her gun at me. There was every natural reason in the world for her to be at peace, and not me. But it was the other way around. She could tell. I did not have to say a word.

The peacemakers are those who radiate the peace of the Lord. Peace is not just the absence of war. The word peace in Hebrew, **shalom**, is one of the most complex and all encompassing terms in the Bible. It is talking about being safely and wholesomely at rest. Being in God's rest is to be at peace. Peace is not just a superficial tranquillity, indicating that there is nothing going on right now, so it is peaceful. In the Biblical sense of the word, there can be peace right in the middle of a full blown war, right in the middle of the most tremendous conflict you can imagine, right in the middle of a disaster because it is an inward state. Peace is the result of the projection of God's power deep into the depths of our soul, convincing us that nothing in this world can eternally harm us as long as we have Him.

Being at peace with God is being in communion with God. It is having a conscience that is devoid of offense. It is a state of perfection of the heart and is a direct descendant of the pure in heart. Only the pure in heart shall see God face to face. It is the kind of peace that can only come from the presence of God. It is a peace that is there wherever God's presence is, no matter what the external circumstances. It is a peace that is instantly available to any of us no matter what kind of difficulty, no matter what kind of problem, no matter what kind of trial or tribulation we are facing or going through. It is a peace that other people can see reflected in us even as we respond to difficult circumstances.

The Hebrew verb, *to restore*, also comes from the same root as the word for peace. It is one of the most frequently used verbs in the Bible and is used in many places to mean that God wants to bring us (and all creation for that matter) back into harmony, or peace with Himself. It is the root for the word "covenant", and also includes the connotation of being made pure and clean.

When I was a kid, my dad used to tell me: **"Life's circumstances are not nearly as important as your reaction to them.** In the end, life's conflicts and injustices will be remembered in the light of how we dealt with them. What will go down in history, what will go down in God's books, will be our response to life's circumstances. How did we respond when this or that happened?"

This is the way it is in many superficial areas of life. Think of baseball games. Do people remember how every pitch went? No, they don't. They only remember when somebody hits a home run or when something spectacular happens. Do they remember every throw to the first baseman? No, but if he drops the ball they remember it!

If our hearts are pure before God, if His presence and peace are there in our lives, no matter what kind of wild pitch we are served, we will respond in a godly manner. Our natural reaction will be godly, because our innermost being is filled with God and with His power. I used to wish when ugly things happened, or when difficult problems occurred, if only I could have a few minutes to get away by myself to kneel down, pray, seek the Lord, and find out how to respond. It is when I am in an emergency, and I have to make a snap decision right away that what I really am inside is exposed for all to see. Do I fly off the handle or shoot from the hip, or is the peace of God still in control?

This life is a training ground. This life is an opportunity to practice for the reality that is to come. At the end of the Sermon on the Mount it says, *whosoever hears these words of mine and does them..."* The word **hear** implies the connotation of someone who is in direct contact with the Lord, and thus receives the grace to comply with what God says.

> *"Whosoever commits sin transgresses also the law: for sin is the transgression of the law. And ye know that he appeared to take away our sins, and there is no sin in him. Whosoever abides in him does not sin: whosoever sins has not seen him or known him.*
>
> *Little children, let no one deceive you; he that does righteousness is righteous, even as he also is righteous. He that commits sin is of the devil; for the devil sins from the beginning. For this purpose the Son of God appeared, that he might undo the works of the devil.*
>
> *Whosoever is born of God does not commit sin; for his seed remains in him; and he cannot sin, because he is born of God. In this the sons of God are manifest, and the sons of the devil: whosoever does not righteousness and that loves not his brother is not of God."* (1 John 3:4-10)

This is a very intriguing passage that used to bother me a lot. Here the Apostle John is using the word for sin, **hamartia**, and is saying that if we belong to God, we cannot sin. Have you wondered about that one? How in the world can we not sin, yet none of us is perfect and all of us are doing things from time to time that need to be repented of and set right. Some people have taken these verses and built a doctrine of sinless perfection; that once we have this encounter with the Lord, no matter what we do, it is not sin. This is a terrible heresy. Again we need to examine the terms. Language is not constant; it can shift with time. The way that I have come to understand this passage is by looking at the term translated sin. There are several. This term comes from a Greek word that has to do with consistently shooting at the wrong target or goal. It does not just mean "to miss the mark". The person could score a perfect bull's-eye, and it would still be sin (**hamartia**) if the archer was aiming at the wrong target.

The way I have understood this is that if we belong to the Lord, if we have Him inside of us, and He is in control of our innermost being; then we will no longer be shooting at the wrong target. We will no longer have the wrong goals. We will no longer be spending our lives after the love of money, greed, selfishness or feeding our pride. We will not be aiming at fulfilling our own desires. We will be aiming for the righteousness of God. We will be aiming for the perfection of God. We are talking about training and target practice in this life. We may not be hitting the target perfectly or even consistently. Every time we shoot, it may not be a perfect bull's-eye but at least we will be aiming at the right target instead of the wrong target. I believe that this is the sense in which John says that when we are in Christ, we cannot sin. He is talking about our goals and ambitions, not absolute sinless perfection overriding our humanity.

There is a certain sense in which we will never get 100% on every math test. We will never be able to perfectly remember everything we said or did. I can tell someone to meet me at 5:00 a.m. and forget and not get there because I am human. Or, I can deliberately try to mislead someone and tell them I will be there when I am not even intending to go. Here are two situations that are as different as apples and oranges. The one is due to my humanity; the other is a deliberate transgression that will interrupt my intimate fellowship with God and definitely needs to be repented of before God and the person that I deliberately mislead.

Even when I make a human mistake or failing it is still necessary to make rectification before the person that I have offended. If I say to someone, "I will meet you here at 5:00 a.m.", and my alarm clock does not go off, or something happens, and I am not there because I forgot or overslept or was delayed, it is not a deliberate transgression that will separate me from fellowship with God. There is, however, the situation between myself and the individual I have inconvenienced that needs to be cleared up. I need to say, "I'm sorry I didn't make it. This and that happened, and I'll try and do better next time." There is a difference between a willful transgression which will cloud our hearts and interrupt our intimate communion with the Lord and a mistake that comes from our human limitations.

Blessed are the peacemakers, for they shall be called the sons of God. They are the ones who radiate peace because the Prince of Peace is on the throne of their lives. This is the goal. This is what God is after. We are to be His ambassadors. We are to represent Him, and He is the Prince of Peace. When He is in control of our lives, we can face the most difficult circumstance or go through the most awful conflict and His peace will never leave us because He says, "I will never leave you, nor forsake you."

One of the ways God has led and guided me is precisely through that peace. Whenever His peace is interrupted in my heart, when something has affected the presence of God inside of me, I know it is time to get off by myself, on my knees before the Lord and not leave until the Lord has put His finger on whatever is not right. It could have been something I said, did, failed to do, thought, or was planning to do. ***God wants to head us off at the pass and stop us before we can even implement wrong elements into our lives.*** He wants to stop us before those ugly words can even come out of our mouths, before we have to go and straighten out what we said or did. He would like us to be so sensitive to His presence that we can detect it when we are just at the beginning stage of wrong thoughts, feelings, or motivation and allow Him to stop and correct us before we miss His perfect will and end up hurting ourselves or someone else.

If we have already messed things up, our error can still be rectified because those around us, especially our families, all need examples. *My dad used tell me that a human life can never be totally wasted. If for nothing else, it can always serve as a bad example for everyone else!* So even when we are a bad example, our lives can still be used to the glory of God if we are willing to submit to Him and do what He wants us to do; which is to ask for forgiveness and to allow Him to deal with our pride as we go to whoever we have wronged to set it straight. We can many times gain more ground for the Kingdom of God by setting an example of repentance and true submission to God than by anything else we could do or say. *Our mistakes and failures are golden opportunities to demonstrate to those around us what real repentance and submission to Jesus Christ is.*

There are a significant number of people, if not all of us, who would have a problem truly repenting and submitting to God without seeing an example in actual practice. I found that the guerrillas who captured me had no concept of repentance. But when I started admitting when I was wrong, some of them came down from their high horses and started admitting when they were wrong. One of them asked me to forgive him with tears in his eyes before I left. These were the same guys who at the beginning stood there and belligerently said,

"We don't make mistakes. Everybody else makes mistakes, but we don't make mistakes."

Have you ever been around someone who does not make mistakes? I have had parents bring their kids in for counselling and say, "This kid will never admit when he makes a mistake." When I started asking them questions, it soon became evident that the father never made mistakes either! Our attitude will imprint on those who are around us. One bad apple can spoil the whole barrel. One conflictive person loose in a church or work place can sour the atmosphere for everyone else that has to be there. The conflictive spirit they have wreaks havoc all over the place. The reverse is also true. One person generating God's peace can have a profound impact on those all around. A little salt can preserve and flavor a whole container of food.

God's peace is contagious. We can go around infecting people with it just as if we had a transmittable disease. When our attitude is right, it speaks way louder than what we say. If we want to truly be effective for the Lord, we need to have two things right. We need to have our attitude, (or our heart) right, while at the same time our doctrine, (or our mental knowledge), also needs to be correct. But it is definitely better to have someone whose heart is right before God, even if their doctrine is not completely straight; rather than someone whose mental knowledge of doctrine is perfect, when their heart is rotten.

To compare this with aviation, most techniques of good pilotage have to do with obtaining and maintaining the proper flight attitude of the aircraft. You cannot do precision maneuvers or fly a precise instrument approach unless you can control the attitude of the airplane through all three axis. This is especially true in short field flying. Someone who cannot control the attitude of the airplane will overshoot or undershoot and could end up having a serious accident. Fledgling pilots should not go anywhere near a short field until they can dominate the attitude of the aircraft.

On the other hand, it is also necessary to know all about the mechanical systems and about navigation. There are many things that a good pilot needs to know in his head, and he needs to know them so well that in an emergency he will act upon the proper information. There have been tragic accidents because something failed on the airplane, and the pilot could not remember if it had to do with the electrical system or with the hydraulic system, and he disabled the wrong system, causing himself more problems. There have been pilots with lightning reflexes who had an engine failure and shut down their good engine, thinking they were shutting down the one that had just failed. It is not necessarily the gifted person with the lightning reflexes who makes the best pilot in a crisis; rather it is the one who calmly, instinctively, does the right thing under pressure. This holds true in Christianity as well.

When we do not know what to do and are under pressure to make a snap judgment or decision, and we do not have the peace of the Lord, the best thing we can do is stop and seek the Lord and find out what He wants rather than go off and make a quick decision we may live to regret later on.

I would like to suggest that you use the beatitudes like a check list. In every aircraft there are always checklists. There are pilots who think they do not need the checklist; they think that they can do it on their own. Everything goes fine until they forget some important item, like coming in for a landing without putting the landing gear (wheels) down first! Many beautiful (and expensive) airplanes have been crunched into the asphalt, destroying the propeller, damaging the engine, sometimes even generating an explosion or fire, because the pilots forgot this simple procedure.

There are important things that God wants us to check. The Scriptures are clear on this. When someone speaks on behalf of the Lord, whether it be teaching, preaching, music ministry, or whatever, there should be the opportunity for those with spiritual discernment to evaluate what has happened and compare anything questionable with the written, revealed, Word of God. It is not just some hotshot saying, "Thus saith the Lord," and nobody can question him. There are people in every part of the body of Christ who will receive gifts of discernment and wisdom from the Lord. They will normally not be your outgoing charismatic type of personalities. These are people who would rather be in the background, people with true servant's hearts who are not self assertive. They need to be drawn out and their gifts need to be cultivated. Their gifts are important, and they balance the others who are gung ho.

If you are a gifted individual, go over the beatitudes and make sure that what you are doing is in line with Jesus' teaching. Go over the first one. When I use my gift, am I feeding my pride? Is it an ego trip for me to be able to stand up and minister to (or entertain) others? If it is, you are headed for trouble. Sooner or later Satan will trip you up, and you will fall flat on your face. Is your gift in submission to the Lord, to do His will and only His will, Do you use your gift with fear and trembling? You do not want to hold back anything that God wants to express through you, but at the same time, you do not want to say anything more than what He wants. Or are you using your gift to play games and to impose your will on others?

There are people who use their God-given gifts to play spiritual parlor games. This is not what they are for. I have been to prayer meetings where there was a, "Can you top this?" spirit and many were on an ego trip. Even leadership can fall into the trap of using a, "Thus saith the Lord," approach when they really want to impose their own will on somebody else. Guess what happens when this kind of thing develops? The glory, power and blessing of the Lord start leaving. What begins in the spirit should not end in the flesh. Worse yet, **Satan can come in with a spirit of deception and substitute the true spirit for a false spirit, and those that are promoting their own glory will not even know when the Spirit of the Lord left them.** This happened to King Saul. He ended up consulting the witch of Endor!

In Jeremiah's day there were numerous false

prophets prophesying whatever the people wanted to hear. Nobody wanted to listen to the true prophet any more because it was uncomfortable. I have a friend who says that although one of the main goals of the church is to comfort the afflicted, if the ministry of the church does not afflict the comfortable, it will ultimately lose the blessing of God.

Blessed are those that mourn, for they shall be comforted. Are you using your gift out of a soft, contrite, humble heart before the Lord, sensitive to the concerns and needs of those around you, sensitive to your own need to be led by God's Spirit? Or do you feel self-sufficient because you are so educated, qualified, or talented?

Blessed are those who hunger and thirst for righteousness, for they shall be satisfied. Do you hunger and thirst for being and doing what God wants; for treating other people right. Or do you just want to be treated right yourself? Do you get your feathers ruffled when somebody doesn't treat you right? Or are you filled with a hunger and thirst for treating other people justly? When Jesus is in control, " how am I being treated..." is no longer important, but rather, "how am I treating others?"

If you think, "I didn't treat that person right. I didn't do right by them." If that bothers you, and you cannot wait to set it right or you're worried that someone may have misunderstood something you said, or you had a word for somebody, and you did not give it to them properly, or you said more than what the Lord laid on your heart; if those kinds of things bother you, then you are on the right track, because you are using your gift out of fear and trembling before the Lord. If you get worried and afflicted when someone does not treat you exactly right, you are still in trouble, and there are a lot of things that still need to be straightened out in your life.

Blessed are the merciful, for they shall obtain mercy. If you have to correct someone, are you doing it in mercy? Are you thinking, "That could have been me. How would I want to be treated if it were me?" Are you filled with forgiveness, or are you ready to rap somebody's knuckles just because they rubbed you the wrong way.

It all boils down to this: ***Blessed are the pure in heart, for they shall see God.*** Are we using our gifts out of a pure heart, or are our hearts clouded? God's end purpose in giving us natural and spiritual gifts and abilities is that we might bear good, wholesome fruit in abundance. The tree that does not bear good fruit will be cut down and burned regardless of its lush, exquisite foliage.

Another thing we need to realize is that Satan will also try to communicate with us. When Jesus fasted and prayed for forty days in the wilderness, the Bible does not relate what God said to Him. It just says that He was baptized by John the Baptist, that the Holy Spirit descended upon Him like a dove, and that the Spirit led Him out in the desert to be tempted (see Matthew Chapter 3). While He was out in the wilderness, Satan came along and began to tempt Him. Be assured that the temptations Satan used were world-class temptations. After all, he was trying to tempt Jesus Christ. The Devil said, "Are you hungry? Then turn these stones into bread and eat."

What could possibly be wrong with turning those stones into bread? It was a "good idea", right? Jesus did miracles later on and multiplied bread and fish and fed people, so why couldn't He feed Himself? There are at least two key things wrong with this line of reasoning that we need to look at. The first thing wrong with it is that the idea did not come from God the Father. Jesus said He was here only to do the will of His Father in heaven. This "wonderful" idea (to turn the stones into bread) originated from Satan. Satan will try to supply us with "good" ideas on how to use our gifts; but if the idea does not come from God the Father, then it is not a good idea. Jesus answered him, quoting Scripture. *It is written, 'Man shall not live by bread alone, but by every word that proceeds out of the mouth of God (the Father).*

There is a second point that also is very important and has to do with the first one. Jesus never, ever, used His gifts to obtain things for Himself or to exalt Himself. He could have, but He chose not to. **If we focus our gifts on exalting and blessing ourselves, we will short circuit the blessing and power of God.** We will receive whatever we can humanly obtain, and no more. **When we are attacked and slandered, if we focus our gifts and abilities on defending ourselves, or if we start taking the law into our own hands; we will get whatever de-**

fense we are capable of coming up with, but we will not get God's defense. If we are stirring up and muddying the waters, we cannot expect the clear, clean cut, intervention of God on our behalf.

So Jesus was tempted to implement a "good idea" that originated from Satan, not from God the Father. Jesus recognized that a "good" idea that comes from Satan is not a good idea. Jesus also demonstrated that He was not going to use His gifts to bless Himself. After He was tempted, the Scripture says that the Father sent angels to minister to Him and to supply His needs. God will supply our needs. We do not have to take our gifts and try to supply our own individual needs. That is not what our gifts are for: they are to edify the collective body of Christ (His Church). (Ephesians 4:11-13)

It is tragic. There have been powerful gifts of evangelism given to individuals with power from God to persuade men to turn to God; but if the evangelist uses his gift to persuade people to give money to himself and to "his" ministry, the next thing you know, the salt has lost its savor, and it is being trampled underfoot by men.

Satan can quote from the Bible too. He took Jesus up to the top of the temple and said, *If thou art the Son of God, cast thyself down, for it is written, He shall give his angels charge concerning thee, and in their hands they shall bear thee up lest at any time thou dash thy foot against a stone.* Satan will quote Scripture. He will try anything to appeal to our pride. When he quotes Scripture to us we need to identify the source of the message. Just the fact that it is a Bible reference that can be pulled out of context and applied, does not mean that God is speaking to us. It has to really be God. Jesus answered him with another Scripture. *"It is written again, Thou shalt not tempt the Lord thy God.* Satan wanted Him to say, "Ok, I'm Superman. Here I go off the pinnacle of the temple." **God is not looking for superstars. He is looking for the humble and contrite in spirit who tremble at His word.** (Isaiah 66:2)

Jesus did not use His gifts to build His own pride. When He did something miraculous; when He healed somebody or even when he raised a little girl from the dead, He would say, "Don't tell anybody. Give the glory to God but don't say it was Me." This contrasts sharply with some of our modern day ministries dealing in "signs and wonders".

The last temptation was, "I'll show you all the kingdoms of the world. Just bow down and acknowledge me, and they're Yours. You don't have to die on the cross. You don't have to give Your life. You can have it all without any sacrifice, pain, or suffering." Satan is still out there offering us that temptation. You can have everything. You're a son of the King. Nothing is too good for you. You don't have to die to yourself. You don't have to pay a price or suffer. You can have everything. Just name it and claim it because you are a King's kid. Jesus rejected that offer and continued His walk in humility. He said, *Foxes have holes, and the birds of the heaven have nests, but the Son of Man has not where to lay his head."* He said, *And whosoever does not bear his stake (cross) and come after me cannot be my disciple.*

There are lots of people out there calling themselves disciples of Christ, claiming to be sons of God, but the ones who are truly the sons of God are those who will take up their cross and follow the Lord wherever He goes. But He says, *My yoke is easy and my burden is light.* His cross is a joy because nothing can compare with the peace He can give.

Gods peace is a direct result of the projection of His power. Think of the tremendous power that holds the universe together, yet this is just a tiny fraction of His might. His power is available to the sons of God; power that can enable them to project, to radiate His peace. The day is coming when Jesus Christ will be revealed in all His glory. The Bible says that all creatures groan and strain waiting for the manifestation (unveiling) of the sons of God (see Romans 8:19-23). When that great day comes, God's sons won't just radiate peace; they will enforce peace. All creation will be brought back into harmony with God, and we (His sons) will be joint-heirs with Jesus Christ. (Romans 8:17)

Blessed are the peacemakers, for they shall be called the sons of God. What do people call you? What does God call you?

"For if ye live according to the flesh ye shall die, but if through the Spirit ye mortify the deeds of the body ye shall live. ***For all that are led by the Spirit of God, the same are sons of God.*** *For ye have not received the spirit of bondage to be in fear again, but ye have received the Spirit of adoption of sons,*

*whereby we cry, "Abba, Father!" For the same Spirit
bears witness unto our spirit that we are sons of God,
and if sons, also heirs certainly of God and joint-heirs
with Christ, if so be that we suffer with him that we
may be also glorified together with him.*

*For I know with certainty that the sufferings of this
present time are not worthy to be compared with the
coming glory which shall be manifested in us. For the
earnest hope of the creatures waits for the manifestation of the sons of God. For the creatures were subjected to vanity, not willingly, but by reason of him
who has subjected them, with the hope that the same
creatures shall be delivered from the bondage of corruption into the glorious liberty of the sons of God."*
(Romans 8:13-21)

Let us pray:

Heavenly Father, we want You to call us Your
sons. Lord, clear away all our own ideas that we
have about ourselves. We want to know what You
think about us. We want to know who we are in
Your eyes. Can those who are around us see You
in us? Is Your character imprinted on us? Are
we each and every day becoming more and more
like you? Or are we like a fruit tree that is rotten
at the core, just producing scraggly little fruit that
gets worse each year? What kind of fruit are we
producing?

Lord, help us to produce healthy, wholesome fruit.
Help us to lead others to You and then see them
go on to a healthy, wholesome walk with You; so
that they in turn can produce good fruit; so that
the world can look at us and see Your image in

us, which will inspire them with hope and plant a desire for You in their hearts; so that we will be tantalizing to the world just like a beautiful, delicious apple on a fruit tree that anyone would be delighted in eating, rather than when they get hold of some of us and take a bite, they spit it out and turn away because some of those claiming to be Your representatives are so rotten and full of worms that no one can stand to partake of what they are offering in Your Name.

Lord, help us. We repent of all the things that we have done our own way, of trying to do Your work our way, of all the mistakes we have made and the errors we have perpetrated, and of the wrong attitudes we have expressed that we have not repented from, of all the things we have done in Your name that were not really in Your name but in our own name. Lord, we want to get back to the cross, back to letting You pick the good ideas, back to using our gifts for others to bring them into a proper relationship with Yourself, to edify Your body.

Lord, please deliver us from using the gifts and abilities that you have given us to build our pride, our ego, our name, or even the name of our collective group. Please deliver us from using the gifts you have given us to line our own pockets or to raise up our own little kingdoms in your name. We want to use our gifts to exalt Your Name; we want to lift You up so that You might draw all men to Yourself. In order to reach others and rescue them from the kingdom of darkness, sacrifices are involved; but You tell us that to obey is better than sacrifice. Please deliver Your people from sacrificing things You never told them to sacrifice. Let our sacrifices be pleasant in Your sight, that we may sacrifice only that which is pleasing and agreeable to You.

Lord, we wish that those who are in the world around us could look at us and say, "They surely must be the people of God, because look at the blessing. Everything they put their hand to prospers. I wish I could have that blessing. I wish I could be like them." That they will be drawn to us and to You. Lord, please give us Your grace, which is really Your power so that we might truly win the battle in Your Name. We are tired of trying to function in this world without Your power, without Your peace. We want to follow behind You, Lord and witness the power of Your presence in us, your people, overcoming the enemy. We want to go in and possess the land in Your name. We want to see the restoration, the purification of Your people, of Your church. We want to win those in darkness away from the tentacles of the enemy. We want to see this nation return to You. Use us, Lord. We want to be a small part of Your great Master Plan. Amen.

Chapter Six

Putting Satan to Flight

Blessed are those who suffer persecution for righteousness' sake, for theirs is the kingdom of the heavens.

THE PROMISE ON THE END OF THE EIGHTH BEATITUDE is exactly the same as that on the end of the first one. It is as if God designed this whole series of attitudes, promises and blessings to be a loop, and for us to just go around and around within the Beatitudes, like going around and around up a spiral staircase.

I have found that the Beatitudes are an excellent check list: When something is wrong in my life, or I need to evaluate my performance in a given area; when I try to search for discernment, a good place to look to make sure my life is on a solid footing is the Beatitudes. I need to periodically check to see whether what I am doing is motivated out of pride or out of a humble heart; to see whether I really want my own way by taking the law into my own hands, or if I am truly submitted to the Lordship and will of Jesus Christ. Is the Holy Spirit shining God's truth into my heart and softening it? Or is my heart hardening? Do I hunger and thirst for righteousness, for doing and being what God wants, or is there some other motivation in my heart? Am I truly interested in treating other people the way I want God to treat me, with a merciful attitude, or is there a root of bitterness beginning to develop in a given relationship or area? Above all, is the peace of God in my heart? Because if it isn't, and I sense that the peace of God has left my heart, the best thing I know to do when this happens is to get down on my knees until the Lord shows me what is needed to regain His peace, to be willing to take whatever steps that He would outline to me.

Doing and being what God wants will bring persecution. It will bring opposition from the enemy. Listen to the ninth beatitude:

Blessed are ye when men shall revile you and persecute you and shall say all manner of evil against you falsely for my sake. Rejoice and be exceeding glad, for great is your reward in the heavens; for so they persecuted the prophets who were before you.

One of the best signs and certain evidence that you are where God wants you to be is if you are receiving persecution. One of Satan's key tactics is to foment lies and rumors. Satan is an expert at getting lies and rumors going. If he can get us suckered into defending ourselves against the lies and rumors; get us defending **our** reputation, then he can get the upper hand, because he can get us to quit hurting him and start defending something that is ours; something that we should have placed on the altar before the Lord long ago. If we have truly entered the spirit of the Beatitudes and have entered the Kingdom of God through the narrow gate, our pride and our desire for reputation should have been left way behind.

It is easy to listen to the Beatitudes. They are lovely; they sound wonderful. There is something inside of us that says, "Yes, that is the way it is. This is the way my personal relationships should be." But when we put it into practice, it is like the scroll that the prophet Ezekiel was asked to eat; sweet in his mouth, and bitter in his stomach. Again, the Apostle John in Revelation Chapter 10 was asked to eat the same type of scroll, or message. The Sermon on the Mount is that way: it is sweet in our mouth, but it can be bitter in our stomach as we digest it and put it into practice.

It is the hearing of Jesus' teaching that starts us on the path to the blessing. Therefore, whosoever hears these words of mine and does them, I will liken him unto a prudent man, who built his house upon the rock... Remember that word for house has a double meaning. It can mean household and family as well as the physical four walls and a roof. So, the Lord is giving an example of a house (or of a family) that was built on the rock. The rain came down and the streams rose, the winds blew and beat against that house, yet it did not fall because it had its foundation on the rock. It is only by putting on Jesus' attitudes, His life, His heart; by implementing these things through the power and presence of His Holy Spirit within us; by becoming a living example of Jesus and His message, that we build our house on the rock.

I was taught by a well-meaning Sunday School teacher that just to believe in Jesus was to have my house on the rock. That is a good start, but the Bible says that even the demons believe, and they tremble with fear (see James 2:19). But they do not live according to the Beatitudes, and they do not have the blessing. They are under a curse. It is not enough to just believe facts about God in our heads in order to have our house founded on the rock: we have to hear Jesus' words in order to put his message into practice. We will make mistakes along the way, and when this happens we have to go back to the first beatitude and be willing to admit our mistakes, forsake our sin, and leave our pride behind. We must resubmit the problem areas of our life to the Lord and ask Him to do a cleansing work within us, starting from the depths of our heart, to purge us of everything which is not right and to give us a hunger and thirst to be what He wants us to be and to do what He wants us to do.

Being is more important than doing. We are in a world that likes to do things, but God's message to us is that He wants us to be a certain kind of people. All of the things that we can do for God will come to an end. Paul says that all these things will come to an end, but there are just three things that will remain: faith, hope and charity, which is the love of God (see 1 Corinthians Chapter 13). They all have to do with Jesus Christ because He is the source of all three. It is our faith in Him, our hope in Him, and it is the kind of love that only He can plant in us: these are the only things that are going to endure forever.

It is very difficult to live the Ninth Beatitude; to get to the place where "friends" can slander us, and we can be in the middle of a full-blown attack from the enemy and still be able to continue on track along the course that God has led us to take without wavering, and all the while to genuinely rejoice that we are receiving this kind of attack! This is not always the case in my life. A lot of times, when the enemy is attacking, and I know the Lord wants me to rejoice, I try to put a smile on my face, but I do not really feel like rejoicing inside. You want to know what I have found? When I do not feel like rejoicing because Satan is attacking and slandering me, it is because there is something that is still mine that I am subconsciously clinging to that I am afraid I am about to lose. It's MY reputation that is on the line, it's MY ministry, it's MY family; anything that is still mine and has not been placed on the altar of total commitment to Christ will take away my capacity to rejoice in the Lord when I am under attack. Jesus said, *For whosoever desires to save his life shall lose it, and whosoever will lose his life for my sake shall find it.*

It is defending what is "mine" that has most often caused me to stop pressing the enemy the way God wants me to press him and to start defending myself instead. Then Satan is able to obtain enough time to marshal his defenses back up and regroup and then does he ever counter-attack! It is very subtle. He will try and get us to react by provoking us. He will try and get a reaction out of us by testing, probing for and attacking any area that is not totally submitted to God.

Let's turn to the book of James. I want to quote you one of the most misinterpreted Bible verses that I know of. Have you heard someone, (or maybe you've done it yourself) quote this verse to the devil when you are in trouble, and he is attacking: *"Resist the devil, and he will flee from you."* If we back up a few lines we find it says in James 4:6,7: *"...God resists the proud, but gives grace to the humble. Submit yourselves, therefore, to God. Resist the devil, and he will flee from you."* That little bit about resisting the devil and seeing him flee from us is contingent upon at least two conditions. The first is that we must be humble (the poor in spirit), and the second is that we must submit ourselves to God (the meek). These are precisely the first three beatitudes. These are the necessary requirements for us to be able to resist Satan and cause him to flee from us.

Friends, I have seen lots of "Christians" trying to resist Satan, and instead of fleeing from them, he turns around and nails them. I have seen this happen often on the mission field, and it has even happened to me a time or two. I have picked myself up bruised and battered and tried to figure out what went wrong. **Satan will try and attack us in any area of our**

lives that is not submitted to God or any area where pride is developing. These are prime targets that he will look for.

If we are spiritually asleep and are not being effective and fruitful for God, Satan will continue to gently, suavely tempt us further and further away from God, but he will not overtly oppose us. Satan will not waste his limited time and resources doing that. But the minute we start to become effective for God, the instant that God begins to have His way in our lives, as soon as the character of Jesus Christ starts to be formed in us, when we start to tap into the unlimited power and authority of Christ and become strong enough to take on an enemy stronghold in the name of the Lord, then Satan has to do something or else he will lose and lose big.

He does not really have good defenses. When the children of Israel under orders from the Lord, marched around the walls of Jericho blowing the trumpet; God brought the enemy defenses down.

When God brings down the walls of an enemy fortress, we can take everything that he has away from him. *The only real way Satan has of counter attacking is to try and probe around and find something that we have kept for ourselves.* Do you remember what happened after the battle of Jericho? At the next battle, what happened? There was a terrible defeat and the children of Israel were driven back. They could not understand why they had had this tremendous victory, and now, all of a sudden they were running from the enemy and the enemy was slaughtering them. It came back to the fact that one of their men had taken, according to the book of Joshua, *a goodly Babylonish garment and two hundred shekels of silver and a wedge of gold of fifty shekels weight* and buried them in the floor of his tent from the spoils of battle that were supposed to have been given totally over to the Lord. Achan caused the entire group to lose God's blessing.

This is what happens if we take for ourselves that which has been dedicated completely to the Lord. Symbolically that Babylonian garment represents the confused human reasoning (justification and deceit) that he was trying to cover his sin up with and silver exemplifies redemption in the Bible. So Achan (meaning "trouble" in Hebrew) was trying to redeem his family (provide for them in the "Promised Land") man's way, with something other than obedience to God, and he ended up getting everyone into trouble instead. **One individual with a rotten heart can bring disaster on an entire group.** God's blessing only returned after Achan and his entire family were removed from the camp and stoned to death.

If we back up a bit in James, to chapter 3 verse 13, it says, *Who is wise and ready among you? let him show out of a good conversation his works in meekness of wisdom.* As we read this you will begin to realize that James has studied the Sermon on the Mount.

> "*But if ye have bitter envying and strife in your hearts, boast not and do not be liars against the truth. This wisdom is not that which descends from above, but is earthly, natural, diabolical. For where there is envy*

and contention, there is confusion and every perverse work.

But the wisdom that is from above is first pure, then peaceable, modest, benevolent, full of mercy and of good fruits, not judgmental, unfeigned. And the fruit of righteousness is sown in peace unto those that make peace." (James 3:14-18)

We discovered something among the many home prayer groups and churches that I have had the opportunity to minister in over the past twenty years. As a rule, the ones that went after power instead of godliness; (all they seemed to be interested in were gifts of power, signs, wonders and miracles) bit the dust in the middle of some scandal, or got further into error, or came under the control of someone who used their spiritual gifts to simply manipulate or milk other people. But the ones that sought unselfishly to do the will of God with a pure heart, became motivated to reach out and help other needy people, some of whom also did the same, starting a chain reaction of God's blessing. Not only were they blessed of God, but they also received the power that these others were looking for and couldn't seem to manage to retain.

Verse 17 again, **But the wisdom that is from above is first pure, then peaceable, modest, benevolent, full of mercy and of good fruits, not judgmental, unfeigned. And the fruit of righteousness is sown in peace unto those that make peace.** Along with righteousness comes the power of God. If we had time we could do a study on this term, **righteousness**, from beginning to end, and see how many times throughout the Bible it is linked to manifestations of the genuine, authentic power of God. God does not pour His power out on the unrighteous (except in judgement). If you want to see the power of God manifested in your life, you must seek virtue and rectitude before the Lord. If you want to be used as a vessel, as a conduit for the Holy Spirit, your heart has to be pure before God, otherwise you stand in grave danger of receiving some other spirit, of getting hooked in some phase of Satan's deception and getting sidelined or sidetracked or of even leading many others astray.

> *"Where do the wars and disputes come from among you? From here, that is to say, of your lusts which fight in your members? Ye covet and have not; ye murder, and have envy and cannot obtain; ye fight and war and have not that which ye desire because ye ask not. Ye ask and receive not because ye ask amiss, that ye may consume it upon your pleasures. Ye adulterers and adulteresses, know ye not that the friendship of the world is enmity with God? Whosoever therefore that desires to be a friend of the world, makes himself the enemy of the world."* (James 4:1-4)

Now remember that James is writing to people who are supposed to be Christians. Yet he is addressing conflicts and quarrels and even murder in what is supposed to be Christendom!

> *"Do ye think that the scripture says in vain, The spirit that dwells in us lusts to envy? But he gives greater grace. Therefore he says, God resists the proud, but gives grace unto the humble. Submit yourselves, there-*

fore, to God. Resist the devil, and he will flee from you." (James 4:5,6)

This verse sums up the victories that we have won over demonic forces in Colombia. This has been the key promise that God has used in our lives. We have had engagements directly with powers of darkness. We do not have to be completely perfect, but we do have to be submitted to God in every area in order to win. We have to be honest before God and be willing to admit our faults and failures rather than cover them up when God's truth exposes things that are out of place in our lives. When our brother has something against us we have to be willing to go with a humble attitude and do what is necessary to set it right.

It is important that we stick together with those that God has placed along side of us. If Satan can divide us, he can conquer us. He likes to divide and conquer. He likes to attack our character, our integrity, and then question all the virtues that God is building in our lives. If we have not truly died to the old man, we will react and start defending ourselves. When we put energy into defending ourselves, Satan will get a second wind and be able to regroup, and we may not be able to win the battle or obtain the victory that we were trying for. I have seen this happen many times. As we have been going through with our crusades in Colombia, each one has been a battle with demonic forces before we were really able to get into that high school and clearly present the gospel to those thousands of young people or before we were able to get into that city and be able to preach in the churches, or before we were able to get permission from the civil authorities.

Satan does not give up ground like that without a fight. He does not want to lose territory. He does not want to lose those whom he has in bondage. He wants to try and take as many people down with him as he can and frustrate God's purposes. Maybe he thinks somehow that if he does that, God will let him off the hook. I don't know. But he is not only continuing his full fledged rebellion against God, he is trying to get as many people with him as possible. He plays for keeps. When he manages to delude people and sell them a bill of goods, and they die that way, it is a very serious situation. We are all responsible for the truth that we have.

Listen to what James says next:

> *"Draw near to God, and he will draw near to you. Cleanse your hands, ye sinners; and purify your hearts, ye double minded. Be afflicted and mourn and weep; let your laughter be turned to mourning and your joy to heaviness. **Humble yourselves in the sight of the Lord, and he shall lift you up.**"* (James 4:8-10)

This: *"humble yourselves in the sight of the Lord, and He shall lift you up,"* comes in the context of spiritual warfare. This is another verse that is quoted out of context all the time as if it should stand alone. But it comes sandwiched right in the middle of how to stand, resist the devil, and put him to flight.

Verse 17 at the end of the chapter says:

"Therefore sin is still in the one that knows to do good and does not do it."

Friends, it is possible for us to do battle in the name of the Lord, to win victories and be able to push back the powers of darkness. It is also possible to take things away from the enemy, to bind the strongman and take what is in his house (starting with the people he holds hostage). If the Lord is giving us orders to go into battle, and we do not fight, it is really sin.

I would like to briefly share a couple of the encounters that we have had on different occasions in Colombia. Satan is very subtle. He will try to get our attention diverted. He will try and make you think that you do not have time to go after the demon that is possessing some person because it will take too long. Maybe you would have to spend weeks praying and fasting in order for that particular demon to come out. You better just leave it alone and go onto something easier. But the Lord can give us wisdom and victory in each and every circumstance.

One time we were leaving for a crusade and were just going out the door. We had tickets to get on an airplane and there were thousands of miners waiting for us down at an emerald mining district. Along came a Catholic priest to the door with a man who was obviously demon-possessed and dropped him off on our doorstep requesting help. The thought went through my mind, "Oh no. We don't have time to deal with this." Then as I reflected in prayer, I thought, "what does God want us to do?" We began to pray that this man would be able to be in his right mind long enough to be able to tell us what he wanted. That is exactly what happened. He came out of his demonic manifestation, and we spoke with him. He said, "Please help me. These things are trying to kill me. They are hurting me." So I said, "Do you want to submit your life totally to God? Do you want to reject the devil and all of his works?" And he said, "Yes!" I said, "Do you want to place your life under the control of God's Holy Spirit?" He said, "Yes!" That gave me an inspiration. I figured that if the Holy Spirit went in, the demon was going to have to come out.

We were praying and did not seem to be going any where when all of a sudden a thought came into my mind to anoint him with oil. So I asked for some oil and I put a little bit on my finger and reached out to touch him. The minute my finger touched his forehead, that was the end of the demon. There was just this stench and a scream as it came out. My wife was standing in the door, and she said it was the strangest scream because it did not just keep coming from his mouth but went right past her out into the street and disappeared. We went and got on our plane and had a wonderful set of meetings. But I thought, "Satan just sacrificed one or more of his guys. He probably sent that demon over here to see if he could get us to miss the plane, knowing full well that the demon probably would not be able to stand against us if we took it on in the name of the Lord. (We had already had victories over others.) But Satan thought it was worth losing one of his guys, if he could stop us or delay us long enough to prevent us from getting on that airplane and make us miss our opportunity to preach to all those miners.

I found another Bible verse that is often misapplied and that is when Jesus comes down off the mountain of transfiguration, where Moses and Elijah appeared beside Him and Peter, James and John were with Him. The other disciples were at the base of the mountain trying to cast out a demon from a child, but they could not do it. Jesus came down and cast the unclean spirit out. Then the disciples asked Him why they could not cast that demon out. The Bible has this reply from the Lord: *"That kind can only come out through prayer and fasting."* The type of prayer that is talked about is not necessarily a long, drawn out affair. The Lord tells us to not pray like the pagans with many words and empty phrases (Matthew 6:7). The word means communication with God or hearing from God in terms of a right relationship with God the Father.

What I believe the Lord is saying here is that this kind comes out only by hearing and receiving orders from God the Father as to what we are to do. You cannot come up with a neat formula to drive it out. We have to hear from God as to what He wants us to do. If He tells you to fast, then fast. But if He doesn't... (see Isaiah Chapter 58). Satan has pulled this one on us lots of times. Whenever we would get up against a severe demon, someone in our group would always say, "Let's forget this and do something else because we don't have time to fast for two weeks." Jesus fasted at the beginning of His ministry, but on this particular occasion He did not fast, He just cast it out. But He also said He did not come to do His own will. He did not come to speak His own words, He did not come to do His own thing. He came to say and do only what the Father said to say and do. We must be in a proper relationship with God if we are to manifest His authority. If we truly learn to walk according to the Spirit of God, in obedience to God, He can give us the specific orders at the specific time in the specific place so that we can win victory after victory after victory over the forces of the enemy.

If we ever slip up and realize that we have made a mistake and that the fire of His presence is not the same as it was before inside of us, we have to go back to the beginning of the Sermon on the Mount, back to the poor in spirit, back to divesting ourselves of our pride and being willing to admit our mistakes both before God and those around us in order for God to be able to continue to bless. Satan would like to tie us up and get us to expend our energy on all kinds of futile things and delay us while he regroups. The Lord wants us to be able to go forward into the heat of the battle, just like the description of that war horse that listens for his orders. In the midst of what looks like massive confusion, we can still follow the precise orders of the Lord and win victory after victory until our enemies are put under the feet of the Lord. This is what He has called us to do.

When it looks like we are out numbered or overcome, if we continue to hang in there, we may be very close to victory. One summer I was asked by a group of Episcopalians to speak at their youth camp.

They sent some of their best young people, the ones who were really moving on with God. There were also some problem kids that nobody knew what to do with for the summer. I decided to teach on the Sermon on the Mount for the entire week. I was coming to the night when I was really going to bring in the net and see what we had caught and who wanted to respond and make a commitment to the Lordship of Christ. It looked like everything was going fine. My message was being well received, and I could feel the anointing and power of the Holy Spirit. Then something happened that totally devastated me.

One besetting sin in my life has been exaggeration. The Lord dealt with me on it when I was in the guerrilla camp. Before that experience, whenever I would exaggerate, and the Lord would convict me of it, I would kneel down and ask the Lord to forgive me, but my pride was too great to go to any of the people I had exaggerated to and say, "You know, that story I just told you was out of proportion and in fact 50% of it was fiction. I'm sorry. The truth is something else." I could not do that. My pride would not let me. So I would say, "Oh Lord, I won't do it again." But because my repentance had not been complete in terms of setting things completely straight, I continued to be dominated by my problem, and I really could not control my tongue.

After I suddenly found myself hostage in the guerrilla camp, the Lord started to cause me to weigh every word that I said. At night, if I could remember I had said some things that were out of line during the day, I would not get any sleep. I would come under intense conviction. I knew I had to have the blessing of the Lord, so there was enough pressure on me to the point where I had to find whoever it was I had exaggerated to, and straighten it out, even when I had twisted things to try to save my own life and prevent my captors from finding out information that could prejudice them against me. So the Lord brought me right back into line in regards to the truth, but at tremendous cost to my pride. It also had quite an effect on my captors, because when they saw me repent of my untruths, it started to impact them in the area of their own pride and made them start to value the truth and come under conviction of sin.

I thought the Lord had cleared up my problem, until I got to that summer camp. I was sitting there during the praise and worship with just a few minutes before I was to go on when all of a sudden Satan started talking to me. You wonder how Satan can talk with a Christian. Well, he can. He can talk with any one of us. He spoke to the Lord. When the Lord was out in the wilderness, Satan came and tempted Him and communicated directly with the Lord. Satan can plant thoughts. He is the accuser of the brethren and that is what he started doing to me in that meeting.

He said, "You thought you were going to do a good job here, didn't you? But you're not. You thought some of these kids were going to come to the Lord, but they're not. You're out of line. What did you just say to that Episcopalian priest at noon?" I thought, "Yeah, he's a scuba diver, and I have a scuba diving license, and I told him a story about scuba diving." And then I thought, "Oh no. I haven't talked to anyone about scuba diving in a long time, and the story I told him about scuba diving was about 50% fact and 50% fiction." I didn't do it knowingly. I just told it the last way I had told it years before. The last time I told it was before the Lord had dealt with me about exaggeration. Even then it was a subtle thing. I would not exaggerate 50% the first time, just 4 or 5% each time I told it and then the next time I told it I would make it a bit better, and then a little more. After telling something about ten times there were whopping lies in it, but I had talked myself into believing my own lies because I had been bringing them up gradually!

So, Satan is telling me, "You deviated from the truth. You exaggerated. God won't bless someone who is lying. You can't possibly expect to stand up there and preach to these kids and have any of them repent. I got you. I got you now, and you're not going to come out of here with anything useful to the Lord."

I felt about an inch tall. I did not want to get up in front of those kids. I just wanted to dig a hole or go out and find some place to have a long time alone between myself and the Lord. Then it occurred to me that I could find the priest and apologize and get it straightened out. But then they announced me. The room was so packed with kids, and he was in the back row, while I was in the front, and there was no way I could get back there, so I had to go up and start speaking. My heart felt like it was as heavy as lead, sitting down at the bottom of my feet some place. I went up there feeling in my heart that I did not have the blessing or the anointing of the Lord.

When I got to the podium, I started out in prayer, and the Lord gave me wisdom as to what to do. I spoke precisely on the importance of the truth and used what had just happened to me as an example. I apologized to the fellow that I had told the exaggeration to right in front of everybody. I faced Satan head on and called his bluff. The Holy Spirit took the consciences of those kids and started to squeeze, and many of them came to a deeper knowledge of the Lord during that time at camp. The Lord broke them wide open. They had a perfect example right in front of them of what they needed to do and how they needed to be honest and sincere and allow the Lord to deal with anything that was not right in their lives. What Satan meant for a route, to win a battle, caused him in fact, to lose the battle. It turned around in a split second, right when I thought it was all lost and was ready to throw in the towel, convinced that nothing could be done. The only thing I could think of was to pray and say, "Lord, I don't know what to do, and if You don't help, we're lost."

This has stuck with me. A lot of the times when I do not know what to preach on, and I do not know what to do (in fact just about every meeting and every time I preach), I like to have a little talk with the Lord and say, "Lord, I don't know what to do. If You do not give me a message and direct me precisely as to what You want said and done, it's useless for me to simply get up and tell a bunch of stories that are going to entertain people, so they can say what a wonderful speaker they had, but nobody will come under conviction of sin or be touched by Your Spirit. Nothing of real eternal value will be accomplished unless You lead the way."

To live the Sermon on the Mount means hand to hand combat with the enemy. It means swallowing our pride and making ourselves of no reputation. It means being able to follow the Lord wherever He leads us. It means submission to the Lord. It means taking on the enemy. But it also means great joy and satisfaction.

Satan does not normally attack unless he is cornered. He is like a snake. Snakes run away from you. I have been all over the jungle, and I know from years of experience that most snakes will always run away from you. The only time they will attack is if they are cornered. One time I was standing on the tail of one and did not know it, but it was still trying to get away from me and never turned around to bite me!

When you start living the way that God wants you to live and start becoming what God wants you to be, you have cornered the devil, and he will have to turn around and attack or else you will cause him serious damage. The Lord will give you a battle plan. He can give you His supernatural joy so that when your reputation is being devastated, and you are being persecuted, when lies and evil things are being said against you, you know what has happened. You know you have Satan in a corner, and you are ready to smash his head, and there will be a tremendous victory where lots of people will be set free and won to Christ if you keep pressing. You have to make a choice to either defend your reputation or keep doing whatever God told you to do. Do not let up on the devil once you have him on the run.

Rejoice in the Lord! The apostle James says:

> *"Humble yourselves in the sight of the Lord and He shall lift you up."*

We do not have to defend ourselves. God can defend us. There may be times when we have to clear something up, but we do not have to make our defense an obsession. We do not have to try to corner someone and say, "So-and-so is going to come and say such-and-such, but I want you to know in advance it isn't so." We don't have to do that. All we have to do is go forward in victory and receive the orders of the Lord. At the darkest moment, when it looks like Satan has us, and he is laughing in our ear and telling us that with all the things we have tried to do for the Lord, they are not going to work out because he has tripped us up somewhere, don't buy it, because a tremendous victory is right around the corner, if we will continue to keep our eyes on the Lord Jesus, listen to Him, and do whatever He wants us to do in that hour of emergency.

Let us pray:

Heavenly Father, we ask for Your victory. We ask, Lord Jesus, that we would be able to follow in Your footsteps and make ourselves of no reputation. That we would be willing to call Satan's bluff every time he threatens us, every time he tries to expose us, or make us lose our standing before men.

Lord, we want the only thing of importance to us to be, what You think of us. Who are we in Your sight? We want to delight in pleasing You, and as we please You, we want to be filled with Your joy to overflowing, so that no attack of the enemy can ever take it away from us. So that when faced with a genuine attack of the enemy involving slander and lies, we can rejoice knowing we have him cornered and that we are being faithful to You, and that this is causing the enemy to become uncomfortable. So we can rejoice in You and go forward, knowing the victory is very near.

I pray Lord, that many would implement the Sermon on the Mount in their lives and put it into practice in order to have their household based on the solid Rock that cannot be shaken no matter what Satan does. That they would be able to claim their family, children and loved ones for You and know that Satan is not going to be able to take them away.

I thank you that we do not have to have large numbers to win the victory over the enemy, but I know that we do have to be pure before You. I pray that we would hunger and thirst for righteousness, for purity, for You, and not seek after power, that we might humble ourselves and allow You to lift us up. Amen.

VIRTUE: The Key to Activating God's Promises

$\mathscr{I}$N ADDITION TO SETTING A STANDARD FOR OUR BEHAVIOR, each Beatitude also has a promise at the end. Those who live the Beatitudes are promised all these things: The Kingdom of Heaven will be theirs, they will be comforted (receive the Comforter, who is the Holy Spirit), they will inherit the earth, they will be filled with righteousness, they will obtain mercy, they will see God, they will be called the sons of God, and they will receive a great reward in Heaven.

These marvelous promises are all conditional. We must comply with God's requirements if we expect to attain His blessing. The themes that are central to the Sermon on the Mount are woven throughout virtually every book in the Bible. The prophet Micah said:

> "He has declared unto thee, O man, what is good and what the Lord requires of thee: only to do right judgment, and to love mercy, and to humble thyself to walk with thy God." (Micah 6:8)

These are the same three central requirements of the Beatitudes. I would like to put this into perspective from a text in II Peter Chapter 1, starting in verse 3.

> "as all things that pertain to life and to godliness are given us of his divine power, through the knowledge of him that has called us by his glory and virtue, whereby are given unto us exceeding great and precious promises, that by these ye might be made participants of the divine nature, having fled the corruption that is in the world through lust." (2 Peter 1:3,4)

As you study the Scriptures, note that most of God's promises are conditional. These conditions need to be met in order for us to be able to claim His "exceeding great and precious promises." Thinking about these conditions, verse 5 says:

> "Ye also, giving all diligence to the same, show forth virtue in your faith; and in virtue, knowledge; and in knowledge, temperance; and in temperance, patience; and in patience, fear of God; and in fear of God, brotherly love; and in brotherly love, charity.
>
> For if these things are in you and abound, they shall not let you be idle nor unfruitful in the knowledge of our Lord Jesus Christ. But he that lacks these things is blind and walks feeling the way with his hand, hav-

ing forgotten that he was purged from his old sins."
(2 Peter 1:5-9)

This is a synthesis of what God wants to do in
each one of our lives. He wants us to participate in
His divine nature. God wants us to experience His
feelings and His thoughts. Our own thoughts and
feelings will betray us sooner or later, but His
thoughts and feelings will bless us and guide us to
victory. He wants to live inside of us and express
Himself in and through us. He wants to give us the
victory, because He is the victory. We have to be
very careful when we claim God's promises that we
have met His conditions. If we lack God's requirements, Peter says that we will be blind and unable
to remember being purged from our old sins. If we
meet God's conditions we will not be idle and unfruitful in our knowledge of Jesus Christ.

Tragically, as we look across the Christian
church, especially the church in North America, it
is very idle and unfruitful. (Not to mention blind
and forgetful). We have vast numbers of people
calling themselves Christians who appear to be doz-
ing when it is time to obey Jesus Christ. They are
interested only in themselves, and in feeling good.
They attempt to use God to obtain what they want
instead of being willing to do what God wants. (see
Rev. 3:14-22)

Starting in verse 5, Peter talks about the conditions for God's promises. *giving all diligence to the
same, show forth virtue in your faith...* Our faith is
the basic commitment that each of us has to Jesus
Christ. What the Bible calls faith is a surrender and

submission to Jesus Christ as Lord and Master of our lives. It is complete dependancy on Him. This will lead us to trust Him and to implement His purpose for our lives to such an extent that we become filled with His presence and begin to reflect His character. I believe that many have fallen into a grave error in Christian doctrine by placing this as the end step (optional of course) of a whole ladder of man-made theology. The superficial theology of just mentally believing or acknowledging biblical facts, repetition of prayers, or mechanical participation in religious rituals, has replaced genuine faith (submission to and dependancy on the Lord Jesus Christ); which is faith in a person, not in a doctrine, a belief, a theology, or some facts. ***True faith is an intimate heart to heart relationship of trust and obedience to Jesus Christ in which we are linked to His overcoming faith.***

In our faith, Peter says we are to show forth ***virtue***. We do not hear too many people talking about virtue in modern English. Virtue means the dynamic of what God approves of, or what God thinks is good. ***The goal of the Beatitudes is that we might develop godly virtue and character so that we will reap the rewards of God's mighty promises.***

Virtue, according to Peter, comes before knowledge. I believe that what God is saying to the church in general right now is that in order to win the great spiritual battle that is raging all around us, our faith must be the rock solid faith of dependance on Jesus Christ as Lord and Master, and we must show forth

virtue in our foundational faith before we add anything else. Virtues are attitudes of the heart which
are a product of being in a right relationship with
the Lord. The Beatitudes are virtues that God wants
to instil in our hearts so that He might bless us with
the fulfillment of His great and precious promises.
The fruit of the Holy Spirit is virtue and this fruit is
much more important than our gifts. There are
many gifted people who according to the Word of
God are going to be lost on the day of judgement.
They will say, "We did wonder works, we prophesied, we even cast devils out in Your name." And
the Lord will reply, "Depart from me you workers
of iniquity, I **never** knew you." (see Matthew 7:21-
23)

The reason that God gives us spiritual gifts and
natural abilities is so that we might produce good
fruit. The Bible says that the Lord looks at the heart.
He is looking for people after His own heart like
King David. Just look at the Psalms to see what
came out of a heart that was in line with God's heart.
Most of King David's Psalms have to do with attitudes and virtues of the heart rather than with complex mental theology. There are many theological
ideas that can be drawn from the Beatitudes or from
the Psalms but their primary purpose is not to teach
complicated doctrine. The Lord is after setting our
hearts right first. **Our hearts need to be right
before our minds can be set right.** God requests that we believe in our hearts (not in our
minds in order to be saved).

> "...the word of faith, which we preach, that if thou
> shalt confess with thy mouth the Lord Jesus and shalt

*believe in thine **heart** that God has raised him from*
*the dead, thou shalt be saved. For with the **heart***
one believes unto righteousness, and with the mouth
confession is made unto saving health." (Romans 10:8-
10)

God's number one priority is to set our hearts
right. Our mouths speak out of the abundance of
our hearts (Matthew 12:34). Notice that according to
this Scripture, the first consequence of believing God
in our hearts is that our mouth begins to confess
Jesus as Lord. The Bible clearly teaches that our
heart (not our mind) has the ultimate control over
our mouth.

"The good man out of the good treasure of his heart
brings forth that which is good, and the evil man out
of the evil treasure of his heart brings forth that which
is evil, for of the abundance of the heart his mouth
speaks." (Luke 6:45)

Virtue comes from the heart, not prima-
rily from the mind. God wants us to relate to
one another from the heart, not just on an intellectual level by trying to mentally analyze everything
that is said and done. It is only when our hearts are
right that He can give us His true knowledge. When
people obtain mental knowledge of Scripture, theology or whatever academic field you want to talk
about, without genuine faith in Jesus Christ and
His virtue in their hearts, the knowledge rarely does
them any good. It feeds their pride and they become puffed up.

Knowledge that is not constructed on the foundation of faith and virtue is a disaster. Just look at

any major university, Christian or secular, and you will see numerous examples of people who have obtained much knowledge without basing it on a solid faith in Jesus Christ. When He is not the foundation, and His virtue is not the primary goal, centers of education become havens for the obnoxious and narrow. They have no room for anyone who does not agree with them and give long dissertations that feed their own egos. Mental knowledge is relatively easy to obtain, but true wisdom comes only from a right (heart to heart) relationship with God. Wisdom has at least two components: 1) We must have the feelings of God in our hearts and 2) We must have the thoughts of God in our minds. *To obtain Godly wisdom, we must first have a restored heart and then a renewed mind.*

Incredible things have happened in the scientific community over the years. Unbelievable errors have occurred when key people refused to admit their mistakes. This has repeatedly caused foundational truths to be swept under the carpet, sometimes for centuries. Almost all of the great breakthroughs in learning have come because someone had to persist, someone had to swallow their pride and continue on when everyone else was slandering them and belittling the truth. When you read the stories of the great men who made advances, not just in Christian theology but in any field, almost all of them were persecuted at the time.

And in knowledge, (show forth) temperance We wonder why we do not have temperance (that is having our behavior under the control of the godly spiritual nature instead of being the slaves of our sinful carnal selfishness). We will do almost any-thing to obtain it. The Christian world is full of how-to-do-it seminars. You can go to these semi-nars and fill your mind with how to do it, but when you go home you still may have very little temper-ance. You may still be a defeated Christian and continue giving in to all the sinful desires and vices of selfish carnality. Temperance has to do with bal-ance and with prudence in all things. Temperance only comes from allowing God to have His way in our lives, from allowing His Holy Spirit to fill us first with His virtue and then with His knowledge. Our will must be aligned with God's will, if we are to have temperance. The Lordship of Jesus Christ is right at the beginning of Christian commitment. It is the threshold we have to get over, the narrow gate into the kingdom of heaven.

> *"Enter ye in at the narrow gate, for the way that leads to destruction is wide and spacious, and those who follow it are many; because narrow is the gate, and confined is the way which leads unto life, and there are few that find it."* (Matthew 7:13-14)

There is a "new" theology out today that says that we can just be "carnal" Christians if we choose. Then at some future point, if we want to, we can make Him Lord of our lives. But it is totally op-tional: we don't have to if we don't want to. Don't let anyone mislead you, we cannot make Him the Lord: He already is the Lord. We do not have power to make Him the Lord. The only thing we can do with our little will is either accept or reject Him as Lord. We can decide whether we are either going to bow before His authority or not. Either He is going to have dominion over our life, heart, mind, and everything we have or else He is not.

Many times with our human limitations we are not capable of consciously surrendering everything we have to the Lord. But the Lord requires that we be responsible only for what we do know about. There will be fresh things that come into our lives (a new possession, a new child, a new situation, a discovered gift or ability) and we must choose whether we are willing to place these things on the altar and lay them at the foot of the cross, or are we going to be our own god and decide what is good for ourselves.

When Peter talks about showing forth in our faith, virtue. This is not necessarily what we think is good. *We must allow the Holy Spirit to sift through our "goodness" and reveal to us what is really good in God's eyes, and what is not, so that we become the kind of people who can spontaneously respond to any circumstance the way God would want us to respond, because He is dominating our hearts and minds. This is what the Beatitudes are all about.* They are about giving God dominion, authority and control over our lives to change us from the inside out, so that we might claim His promises and walk in victory.

The Christian life cannot be intellectually learned. That is not the way it works. This is why many of the seminars and conventions in the church today are not producing godly virtue and character in our lives. We continue to be defeated by the enemy on almost every front because the cart is still in front of the horse. Many of the Christian principles that are being taught are wonderful, most of them are true, but God never intended for us to turn the New Covenant into another Old Covenant of rules and regulations. He wants to live as Lord in our hearts and reign and rule from there, so that everything that goes forth from our hearts will be a spring of living water that originates out of Himself. Then He will be delighted to open our intellectual understanding, so that we might become even more effective and fruitful in His Kingdom. There is a very important place in Christianity for intellectual learning, but unless we go about it according to God's priorities, and not according to our own, our intellectual attainments will feed our pride and defeat God's purposes for us.

The Christian life is unpredictable from our human standpoint in the sense that God can give us a spontaneous reply at the proper moment that we could never have thought up on our own. God can give us a message that we could never have invented by ourselves. God can give us a love for someone else in a moment of crisis that would have been humanly impossible without His presence in our hearts.

His perfect plan for us is not that when we are being defeated and are full of wrong emotions, rebellion, bitterness, and pride, that we have to go off and spend quite a few hours with Him before we can pull ourselves together and come out and face whatever our predicament is. His goal for us when we are in an unexpected crisis, is that He will be in our hearts, and that our response to the obstacle will be His response; that there will be a spring of living water coming up out of us. This is how we can become effective for the Kingdom of Heaven. Look at the things that will follow when we build according to His plans and on His foundation. He is the Rock; He is the only secure foundation.

> ". . . and in temperance (show forth) patience; and in patience, fear of God; and in fear of God, brotherly love, and in brotherly love, charity." (2 Peter 1:6,7)

This word *charity* is the Greek word **agape**, which means sacrificial love, and is not just an emotion. This kind of love is a decision. It is the decision that Jesus made when He died on the cross for us, while we were yet sinners. It is the determination to reach out to others in response to the call of God, no matter what the cost to our pride, ego, time or resources. It is being willing to make sacrifices to reach out to others and show them that God really cares.

> "For if these things are in you and abound, they shall not let you be idle nor unfruitful in the knowledge of our Lord Jesus Christ. But he that lacks these things is blind and walks feeling the way with his hand, having forgotten that he was purged from his old sins. Therefore, brethren, give all the more diligence to make your calling and election sure; for doing these things, ye shall never fall. Because in this manner the entrance shall be abundantly administered unto you in the eternal kingdom of our Lord and Saviour Jesus Christ." (2 Peter 1:8-11)

Notice, that here is another promise. **IF** these

things are in you and abound, you will never fall. Here is a guarantee from God that we can live in victory, and that He will sustain that victory in and through us, *if* we are willing to live His way, build on His foundation, and meet His conditions. The Old Testament is full of examples of what happened to the children of God when they refused to walk after Him according to divine order, when they wanted to live their lives some other way. The children of Israel had all kinds of terrible calamities happen to them when they refused to live according to God's orders.

The epistles of Paul also tie in with the Sermon on the Mount. Paul assumes that the Beatitudes are fundamental to the gospel. He makes many references to the gospel, as if those to whom his letters are addressed should thoroughly understand it, because he had been there and lived it and practiced it in front of them.

*"And the **peace of God**, which passes all understanding, shall keep your hearts and minds through Christ Jesus.*

*Finally, brethren, whatever things are true, whatever things are honest, whatever things are just, whatever things are pure, whatever things are lovely, whatever things are of good report, if there is any virtue and if there is any praise, excercise yourselves in these things. Those things, which ye have both learned and received and heard and seen in me, do, and the **God of peace** shall be with you."* (Philippians 4:7-9)

The gospel of the Kingdom of God, which is the gospel that the Apostle Paul preached, is not always identical to the many gospels that are preached in our present day and age. Some preach the gospel of "prosperity", or the gospel of "name it and claim it." There are others that preach the gospel of "eternal security". These all have some truth, but their promises are only for fully committed disciples of the Lord Jesus Christ.

There are those who preach building their own kingdoms instead of God's Kingdom. There are many gospels out there, competing with the true Gospel of the Kingdom of God. The Gospel of the Kingdom of God is simple: He is the King. Jesus is the King; He is the Lord. There is no other. God says that in the times of ignorance He overlooked, but now He is calling upon all men everywhere to repent (see Acts 17:30). Repent of what? Of going our own way, of being our own god.

Acts 5:32 says that He gives His Holy Spirit to those who persuade Him (JB2000). The construction of the language is exclusive, so in other words it could also be translated: He gives His Holy Spirit only to those who persuade Him. Those who persuade Him that they really want to live in covenant with Him. Those who persuade Him that they really want to be treated and corrected as His sons. If you have the Holy Spirit and do not choose to obey Him, you will quench the real Spirit. The worst part about the tragic story of King Saul was that the Spirit left him, and he did not even know when it left (see Galatians 3:3).

Consider these two cases: Have you ever wondered why David did not lose the Holy Spirit even after he committed murder and adultery? And yet look at what happened to Saul. All Saul did when he was supposed to exterminate those who were in rebellion against God and completely destroy everything they had, sparing nothing, was that he kept their king alive and spared the best of their goods and animals under the pretence that he was going to sacrifice them later to the Lord. He only destroyed that which was weak and despised. Then he went out and set up a monument in his own honor! (1 Samuel 15:7-26)

Saul wanted to be his own god. He wanted to decide both what was going to be done, and when it would happen. The things that he decided seemed good to him at the time. The only problem was that his actions and the things that he saved for himself were not good in God's eyes. When the word of Lord came to him, saying, "What are you doing?", he did not repent like King David did. He did not say, "I'm sorry. I should have paid closer attention to what God said." He did not plead with God to cleanse and restore him. No, he said, "I've been doing everything right. What's the big problem? I'm the king. Can't I decide?" The enemy king had not even been dealt with! Saul had been using his position in the army of God to feed his own pride and to line his own pockets! (see 1 Samuel Chapters 13-15). The kingdom was taken from him and given to a man after God's heart: David.

Even though David wasn't perfect and also made serious mistakes, he sought God with all his heart. David put God first and greatly valued the presence of the Holy Spirit. After his sin, he pled with

God to not take His Holy Spirit from him, and God not only forgave him, but thoroughly cleansed him; God not only restored him to service, but gave him victory after victory over his enemies.

We presently have many leaders attempting to use the Kingdom of God to build their own kingdoms. Instead of serving God's sheep, they have been fleecing the sheep and lining their own pockets. They have been mixing money in with the Word of God. We are coming to a time, and I believe it is at our doorstep, when judgment has begun in the house of God. Everything is going to be exposed for what it is. Those things which are presently being done in secret are going to be shouted from the housetops. Everything that can be shaken will be shaken, because the Lord is coming back for a church that is pure; for a bride that is clean, white and beautiful. Right now, the church is an ugly mixture of man's plans mixed in with God's plans. This has to be straightened out prior to the Lord's return, and it is going to be extremely painful for some. But those who submit to God's discipline, those who allow God to cleanse them from the sin of going their own way, will be given the victory. Jesus Christ will return for a glorious church without spot or wrinkle or any such thing. (Ephesians 5:27)

The Bible speaks of those who *"have washed their long robes, and made them white in the blood of the Lamb."* What is the blood of the Lamb? What does being cleansed by the blood mean? When we talk about the power of the blood and of being covered by His blood, it is not just some mystical term. *Jesus precious blood was not shed so that we can employ a magical formula for doing whatever we want and then justify our evil actions with pious talk about "pleading the blood."* The blood is not a magical term. The Bible says that the life is in the blood. When we are talking about the blood of Christ, we are talking about Christ's life. It is the same blood that He shed for us, so when we talk about His blood we are also talking about His death. This is a term that encompasses both the life and death of Jesus Christ.

> *"For the soul (or life) of the flesh is in the blood, and I have given it to you to reconcile your persons (or souls) upon the altar; therefore the same blood reconciles the person."* (Leviticus 17:11)

When we talk of putting the blood of Christ over us, being covered with the blood of Christ, we are talking about being dead to going our own way and allowing the resurrection life of Christ to live inside of us to lead us, to guide us and to empower us to live a victorious Christian life. We have taken Christ's blood and turned it into a code word for something magical that we can throw out and sound holy, while we continue to do our own thing, to be our own god and to go our own way. This is not what God has in mind at all.

> *"This then is the promise which we have heard of him and declare unto you, That God is light, and in him is no darkness at all. If we say we have fellowship with him and walk in darkness, we lie, and do not the truth; but if we walk in the light, as he is in the light, we have communion with him in the midst of us, and*

the blood of Jesus Christ, his Son cleanses us from all sin." (I John 1:5-7)

In the Old Testament, before offering a sacrifice, the person had to put his hand on the animal before it was killed, before it's blood was shed with an attitude of repentance that said, "I deserve to die. This ought to be me. This is my death. I do not want to ever commit this sin again."

This was the difference between David and Saul. When Nathan the prophet went to David and told him about his sin, David did not say, "I am the king. I can decide. Who me? No, I haven't done anything wrong." He did not try and justify or excuse it. He said, "I have sinned." He rent his garments and fell on his face before the Lord. He asked the Lord to cleanse him and make him whole and the Lord did. There were consequences and chastisement for the sin. There were ugly incidents later regarding his sons that were probably spawned by David being involved in murder earlier on. The prophet said that bloodshed would not leave his house. But God restored King David and left him on the throne of Israel.

God even kept His promises to David that one day one of his descendants would be the Savior and Messiah. He did not sideline David and neither will He sideline any of us for our failures, if we have an open heart before Him. When He points out our inadequacies, mistakes and sin, we need to be willing to repent and ask forgiveness saying, "I don't want to do it again. I want to set it right. I want Jesus to shine the light of His Holy Spirit into the shadows of my heart that I might be cleansed and made whole". But if we say, "Who me?", and try and justify ourselves, we can go the route of King Saul. God can lift the anointing of His Holy Spirit, and if we continue headstrong along our own way, we might not even know when He left.

Peter says that we need to be **giving all diligence** to show forth in our faith, virtue, and in virtue, knowledge; and in knowledge, temperance . . . Notice the part about, "giving all diligence." There is another lie that has been planted in the church, which says that since our salvation is not by works, we do not have to do anything: It is a free gift of God. Then they say, "When is the free gift yours? When you receive 'it'." All of a sudden they are talking about receiving an 'it' instead of a "Him." The "it" is not going to save us; only the "Him" can save us. Only He can do those things which we cannot do for ourselves. This is another definition of God's grace. It is also a definition of His power. God's grace and God's power are not "magical" either. If we do not put our will into it and give all diligence to following Him, and set our heart on going His way, we will become idle and unfruitful in our knowledge of Jesus Christ. To become a victorious Christian takes everything we can put into it, and even that is not enough, because we need Him; His grace and His power. We need to learn to rest in and rely on the Lord, but nowhere does God say that we are not to put our very best into trying to become what He wants us to be. Nowhere does the Bible say that we are called to mediocrity, to just do the least that we can to get by. My father told me, "Make no mistake, believing doctrines cannot save us even if they are true: only Jesus Christ can save us. We must believe Him."

The complete and unshakable assurance of salvation that we have comes only from submitting to His Lordship. If we will not submit to His authority over us, how is He supposed to discipline us when we need it, or control all our life's circumstances to mould us and make us into what He wants us to be? How is He supposed to protect us? How is He supposed to deliver us, if we have retained areas of bondage to the enemy where we do not want His intervention? How is He supposed to keep us from being defeated by the enemy, if we insist on leaving ourselves wide open to attack?

In order to be able to stand, in order to become what God wants us to be, in order to have security for the future, it is essential that we submit to His authority and allow Him to be sovereign in our lives. We must remember that God is a gentleman in the sense that He will not force Himself on us. We do not have to make ourselves perfect, or clean ourselves up to come to God. He is willing to receive us, no matter what kind of problems we have. But we need to get one basic thing straight: who is the boss? Who has the last word? Are we willing to let Him intervene unconditionally in our affairs?

If you go into the hospital for surgery, there are forms to be filled out and signed saying that you authorize the doctor to take any measures he needs to take in order to save your life. If he opens you up and finds something else wrong (other than your original problem that you sought the doctor for), he is authorized to fix that too. Several times when I have been in the hospital, I have had to sign forms that authorize the hospital and the doctor. Once when I did not sign the forms, the hospital refused to treat me. The Lord is this way too. We cannot say, "I'm only going to let You do this much and no more." He might not operate. We might not see His power. We will not experience the fullness of the true anointing of His Holy Spirit, if we are trying to limit Him in our lives.

You cannot have just however much you want. You cannot come to Him and say, "Just solve this problem and no more." You have to be willing to say, "Lord, here I am, and whatever needs to be fixed, You fix it. I will cooperate with You *giving all diligence*." That is the prescription for being able to claim this promise: *"For doing these things, ye shall never fall."* What things? *giving all diligence to the same, show forth virtue in your faith; and in virtue, knowledge; and in knowledge, temperance; and in temperance, patience; and in patience, fear of God; and in fear of God, brotherly love; and in brotherly love, charity.* Not only will we never fall, God promises that we will not be *idle* or *unfruitful* in the knowledge of our Lord Jesus Christ.

There is a big difference between obedience to the law (dead works of the flesh) and the obedience of faith (victorious life in the Spirit). In obedience to the law, we are trying to obey with our own resources. In the obedience of faith we put faith in

Jesus Christ to give us the power (grace through His Holy Spirit) to carry out His will.

I would like you to think to consider whether you are idle or unfruitful in your knowledge of our Lord Jesus Christ. Would you like to be more effective and more fruitful, or do you think that you are effective and fruitful enough? Spend some time alone with the Lord, listening to Him and going over every area of your life, every relationship in your family, with your friends, and even with your enemies. Ask Him to show you where He wants you to be more effective and fruitful for Him. Ask Him to show you how to live the Beatitudes. Ask Him to plant His Beatitudes deep down in your heart.

If the Beatitudes are just in your mind, then when you face an enemy ambush you won't have time to dig them out and figure out how to apply them. That will not work. They have to be planted deep down in your heart, so that they will automatically flow out of your innermost being when you are under attack. This will happen only through practice, through going through crisis after crisis and then evaluating your behavior afterwards with the Lord. You need to ask Him, "How did I do? What would You like to change? How can I do better next time?"

Let us pray:

Lord, King Solomon built a glorious temple out of all the spoils of battle, out of all the booty that King David, his father, took away from Your enemies. Lord, I pray that we also will be able to take things away from the enemy, who has bound up and held hostage vast resources of millions, billions of people that he has caged up in man-made systems of confusion. Lord, that we might understand the way Your Kingdom really works and operates. That we will not just run around and do "good things" our own way, but be willing to do Your things Your way. That we would allow You to come in and circumcise our hearts and with your two-edged sword, cut the control of our fleshly sinful nature; and then with Your fiery finger, write Your commandments on the tablets of our hearts and in our minds. Allow us to participate in Your nature, so that Your feelings and Your thoughts might dominate every aspect of our being, so that You would live in us and be our God and we would be Your people living in intimate communion and fellowship with You. May Your presence and peace shine forth out of us and affect all those with whom we come into contact. Amen.

Chapter Eight

Rebuilding the Ancient Ruins

"All this, said David, the LORD made me understand in writing by his hand upon me, even all the works of this pattern.

And David said to Solomon, his son, Be strong and of good courage, and do it; fear not, nor be dismayed, for the LORD God, even my God, will be with thee; he will not leave thee, nor forsake thee, until thou hast finished all the work of the service of the house of the LORD." (1 Chronicles 28:19,20)

"And the LORD magnified Solomon exceedingly in the sight of all Israel and bestowed upon him such glory of the kingdom as had not been on any king before him in Israel." (1 Chronicles 29:25)

A VERY TRAGIC THING HAPPENED HERE IN THE BOOK OF CHRONICLES. We read how King David, as he was on his death bed, gave his last words or requests to his son, Solomon. At that point in time, Israel was at its zenith morally, and spiritually and was receiving the blessing of the Lord. The Lord had picked Solomon to build the temple and the first book of Chronicles ends with the children of Israel joyfully giving all of their gold and silver and precious stones (of their own free will) for the building of the temple. King David gave all of his own personal wealth, and it says that there was great rejoicing at the thought of building the temple of the Lord.

The second book of Chronicles starts out with the glorious construction and dedication of Solomon's temple which ushered in the golden age of Israel, but this book has one of the most tragic endings in Scripture:

"Moreover, all the princes of the priests and the people increased the rebellion, rebelling according to all the abominations of the Gentiles and poluting the house of the LORD which he had sanctified in Jerusalem.

And the LORD God of their fathers sent to them by the hand of his messengers, rising up early, and sending because he had compassion on his people and on his dwelling place. But they mocked the messengers of God and despised his words and misused his prophets until the wrath of the LORD arose against his people, and there was no remedy.

Therefore, he brought upon them the king of the Chaldees, who slew their young men with the sword in the house of their sanctuary and had no compassion upon young man or maiden, old man, or him that stooped for age; he gave them all into his hands.

Likewise, all the vessels of the house of God, great and small, and the treasures of the house of the LORD and the treasures of the king and of his princes; all these he brought to Babylon.

And they burnt the house of God and broke down the wall of Jerusalem and burnt all its palaces with fire and destroyed all its desirable vessels." (2 Chronicles 36:14-19)

What a tragic ending. What a terrible thing to happen to God's people and to His sanctuary, His temple. Everything was totally demolished. All because God's people became unfaithful. Even though they continued their sacrifices and all their religious practices; even though they went through the motions of worshiping God and felt very self-righteous as they were doing it, they didn't do the will of God. They didn't listen to what God was telling them through His prophets. They didn't really grasp what He wanted when He said that to obey is better than sacrifice.

The temple was in ruins; the walls of Jerusalem completely destroyed due to the disobedience and rebellion of God's people. But God did not leave things in this terrible state of disarray. He raised up a remnant under Ezra to rebuild the temple, and then He raised up Nehemiah to rally the people of God and rebuild the walls of Jerusalem. We are also living in a time when the (spiritual) temple of God needs to be restored, and the (spiritual) walls of God's protection around His people need to be rebuilt. Let us look at what the prophet Isaiah has to say about this:

"And shall say, Clear away, clear away, level the way, take away the stumblingblocks out of the way of my people.

For thus has said the high and lofty One that inhabits eternity, whose name is the Holy One;

I dwell in the high place and in holiness and with him also that is of a contrite and humble spirit to cause the spirit of the humble to live and to cause the heart of the contrite ones to live. For I will not contend for ever, neither will I be always be wroth: for by me is the spirit covered by the body, and I have made the souls. For the iniquity of his covetousness I was wroth and smote him: I hid my face and was wroth, and he went on rebelliously in the way of his heart. I have seen his ways and will heal him: I will lead him also and restore comforts unto him and to his mourners.

I create the fruit of the lips; Peace, peace to him that is far off and to him that is near, said the LORD; and healed him. But the wicked are like the sea in tempest, that cannot rest, whose waters cast up mire and dirt. There is no peace, saith my God, for the wicked."
(Isaiah 57:14-21)

Clear away, clear away, level the way, take away the stumblingblocks out of the way of My people. This is what God wants to do for each one us as individuals and collectively as a body. It is much easier for God to work with an individual here or there, than to collectively raise up an entire body that is going to walk in the way that He wants them to walk. It is even harder, if not impossible, to obtain the perfect cooperation of different church orders or denominations. But there are certain enemy strongholds that can only be taken down when God mobilizes his entire army as a group.

"Remove the stumblingblocks out of the way of My people." That is what He is doing right now. God is now in the business of removing all stumblingblocks out of the way of His people. *If we are willing, God will remove the obstacles in our way that prevent us individually and collectively from becoming effective and fruitful in His Kingdom.* On the other hand, there are those who have put themselves in a gilded cage of their own making or of their particular denomination or group, and love to have it so. The Lord wants to do away with this. He is going to start shaking and rattling the cages until they all come apart. He wants to break the yokes of bondage that have enslaved His people for so long.

Isaiah 58 is one my favorite chapters in the Bible. Listen to this!

> *"Cry aloud, do not hold back; lift up thy voice like a shofar and preach to my people their rebellion and to the house of Jacob their sin."* (Isaiah 58:1)

Whenever Israel was turned away from God, He started slipping in these references to "Jacob", instead of calling them Israel. Jacob means conniver, or supplanter. That is what God's people like to do. We like to connive. We like to think, "What is the least I can do and still be saved? What is the least I can do and still have God's blessing? What is the least amount I can give and still have God bless me financially? What is the least amount of time I can give and still count on God to help me when I need

Him? What is the least amount of service I can do in my church and still feel that I can call on the leadership in case I need help sometime?"

This is the way the natural man goes about things. God wants to turn this around and declare to His people their rebellion. The Bible says that **rebellion is the sin of witchcraft and to break the word of the LORD is iniquity and idolatry** (see 1 Samuel 15:23). We may think that it is not too serious to be rebellious and to break the word of the Lord but they are two of the worst sins that we could possible imagine, because in addition to affecting our relationship with God, they will bring us under bondage to the enemy.

> *"That they seek me daily and want to know my ways, as people that do righteousness and have not forsaken the rights of their God: they ask me of the rights of righteousness and desire to approach God. Why have we fasted, they say, and thou dost not see? why have we afflicted our soul, and thou dost take no knowledge?"* (Isaiah 58:2,3)

Our worship is a bit different today, but we could say, "Why do we come to church, Lord? You haven't healed our land. We paid our tithe, Lord, yet our country is still running downhill." We have gone through the motions of worshiping God, but the thought that comes to my mind looking across North America is that what ought to be the fortress and city of God has become instead, the city of organized religion. **Instead of building the Kingdom of God, we have built incredible religious machinery, much of which actually**

stands in the way of God being able to bless us, deliver us, and heal our land.

All of us are susceptible to this kind of thing. For example on the family level, it is easier to make up a set of rules and regulations to run our families by, than to really be sensitive to the Spirit of God and allow Him to be the true leader of our homes. Reflect on your own household and on your own life and ask God to show you if there are yokes of bondage that you have helped create, that may have stifled the Lordship of Jesus Christ and the anointing of the Holy Spirit in your home, to the point where Satan has been able to wreak havoc with your family. **Many times, as a prerequisite to going forward to victory, we must first be willing to dismantle those things which we have created that God does not like. In the corporate structures of our churches, I am sure we need to do the same thing.** We need to be willing to go over all the traditional structures that we have put into place and see if they are all truly pleasing to the Lord and make sure that there are no yokes of bondage that have been created by human effort that could be holding back the blessing of the Lord.

> *"Why have we fasted, they say, and thou dost not see? why have we afflicted our soul, and thou dost take no knowledge? Behold in the day of your fast ye find your own pleasure and exact your own estates. Behold, ye fast for strife and debate, and to smite with the fist of wickedness: ye shall not fast as ye do this day to make your voice to be heard on high."* (Isaiah 58:3,4)

A lot of churches (and families also) end in splits today. People take off and go different ways. It is easier to find new friends than to reconcile the conflict. Quarrelling and strife is rampant in our families, as well as in our businesses. It is all too easy to have this happen. If there is any danger that we are going to acknowledge the Lordship and authority of Jesus Christ and allow Him to clean and purify our hearts; if there is any danger of truly becoming effective for Jesus Christ, Satan will attack. The first place he will always probe is our personal relationships.

When personal relationships start going haywire, Satan actually uses the man-made machinery that is in place to accelerate the conflict. "Well, you broke the rule that we made. You didn't treat me the way that I treated you. You weren't supposed to do that and you did it anyway." On and on and on. He tries to get our relationships with one another onto an intellectual level of rules and regulations of who did what when, and who said what where, and who hurt who how; instead of the heart to heart flow of the river of life relationships originating in the heart of God.

> *"Behold, ye fast for strife and debate, and to smite with the fist of wickedness: ye shall not fast as ye do this day to make your voice to be heard on high. Is it such a fast that I have chosen? a day for a man to afflict his soul? is it to bow down his head as a bulrush, and to spread sackcloth and ashes under him? wilt thou call this a fast and an acceptable day to the LORD?"* (Isaiah 58:4,5)

For many people that is what coming to church is. It is an obligation, something they force themselves to do in the hope that God will recognize and honor their sacrifice of choosing to go to church, rather than go fishing or whatever.

This is not what God is after at all. If you are still on the level of practicing your religion because you feel an obligation, if it is a great sacrifice for you, then you are in the same boat with the Jew who would do his fasting in sackcloth and ashes in order to appease God. That is the wrong motivation. God is after a change of heart. He truly wants to place in our hearts a joy to be with our brothers and sisters in Christ, so that we might worship and fellowship with Him.

This is what is so hard about parenting. There is a certain amount of discipline required to get our children established according to divine order. But if the only reason the kids go to church is because that is the rule, the day will come when they will be out on their own, and they either will not go at all, or they will be going the rest of their lives out of a wrong motive and may never attain all that God wants for them. If the parents are not filled with the joy, blessing and anointing of the Lord, it is very difficult for the children to obtain them.

Verse 6. *"Is not rather the fast that I have chosen, to loose the bands of wickedness, to undo the ties of oppression, to release into freedom those who are broken, and that ye break every yoke?"*

As Christians, we need to make sure both in our families and in our corporate expression of Christianity, that we are not one of the legalists sitting there, making heavier yokes and more chains for everyone else. That is our human, natural way of doing things. When there is a problem, or an abuse, we make a half dozen more rules to make sure it doesn't happen again and put everyone in more of a straight jacket and take that much more liberty away from the Holy Spirit. God intended for the Jews to be a people who would live in freedom with liberty to express themselves to Him, to worship and honor Him. Over the centuries they added to the books of Moses and came up with an incredible number of rules and regulations, until by the time Jesus came, nobody could do anything without breaking a rule. They would meticulously keep all this and think that by doing so they were serving God, yet the blessing of God had left them long ago. It was to such an extreme that even when Jesus Christ walked among them and healed the blind and raised the dead, doing miracles that they had never seen or heard tell of before in their lives, they still did not give glory to God because Jesus was not interested in all their petty rules and regulations. He had come to share the heart of God with them, and they totally rejected it because it was so foreign to the gilded cage of legalism that they had surrounded themselves with.

We have to be continually on our guard so that the same thing does not happen to us. We need to look for chains and yokes and make sure that we are not the ones creating bondages. We need to make sure we are not saying, "Well, since this happened to me, and I had this negative experience, then I had better make sure that there is no way any one else can get hurt by this, so we will have this and that rule," and thereby we add to the Word of God. At the end of the Bible in the book of Revelation, there is a terrible curse on anyone who would add to or take away from the Word of God.

Obviously there has to be order. Our churches and families are not to be totally uncontrolled. But we have to make sure that it is divine order, the order that God ordaines, and not some other order that we came up with as a substitute for God's order. We have to make sure that we are truly shouldering our God ordained responsibilities. If you are the head of the household, it is your responsibility to be sure that your household is being run according to God's order, and not some other order that you made up or that you learned somewhere. If you are a part of the leadership of a church, it is your responsibility to be sure you are truly participating in God's order and not some other kind of order.

In verse 7 it says,

"Is it not to share thy bread with the hungry and that thou bring the poor that are cast out to thy house? when thou seest the naked, that thou cover him; and that thou not hide thyself from thy brother? Then shall thy light break forth as the morning, and thine health shall spring forth speedily: and thy righteousness shall go before thee; the glory of the LORD shall be thy rereward. Then shalt thou call, and thou shalt hear the LORD; thou shalt cry, and he shall say, Here I am. If thou take away from the midst of thee the

yoke, the putting forth of the finger, and speaking vanity." (Isaiah 58:7-9)

As I travel across this continent, I hear lots of prayers going up in many churches and most people want great things from God. "Lord, heal our land. Lord, heal me when I'm sick. Lord, we don't have enough money. Lord, save our schools." Rarely do I see spectacular, clear cut answers to prayer where the power of God has descended, and there is clear difference between those who are serving God and those who are not. I believe this is because God's conditions have not been met by those who claim to belong to Him. We have not allowed the Lord to do what He wants to do in and through us.

... to share thy bread with the hungry and that thou bring the poor that are cast out to thy house. One time when we were very poor, growing up on a missionary base, my Dad started to apply some of these promises and meet some of the conditions. He had a whole book of all of the promises in Scripture. He would get down on his knees and ask the Lord what He wanted him to do in order to meet some of these conditions and activate God's promises. Dad did some "strange" things for which he was severely criticized.

One of them occurred when we were to have a big banquet for all the government dignitaries who were in charge of the Ministry of Government. The missionaries were about to be kicked out of the country, so the mission was interested in giving the leaders of the government a favorable impression of the mission base. An airplane was sent to fly all the dignitaries from the capital city to the missionary compound. The mission public relations fund was drained to buy food and supplies to put on a special banquet. Everyone got out their best lace tablecloths and china. It all centered around our house, because my dad was in charge of the technical work for the mission, so it was his job to handle the government dignitaries. My mom and some of the ladies who were the best cooks among the missionary wives cooked a special dinner. We took all our living room furniture out and put extra tables in our living room and dining room. But then the Director of our mission called with a report that there was bad weather and the trip had been canceled and put off until next week. So there we were with this exquisite banquet and no invited guests. The Director wanted to know if our family could eat all the food and then pay the public relations fund back!

Dad and Ricardo had just been reading in their Bibles where it said that if the wedding guests who had been invited did not come, you were to go out into the highways and byways and compel them to come in. Ricardo felt that this was what we should do. There were a lot of poor neighbors outside the gates of the mission compound. We were not supposed to be working with them because we had just been chartered to work with Indians, and a lot of our missionary co-workers felt that if we worked with these needy Spanish speakers, we would jeopardize our government contract. So we had just been sitting there allowing horrendous need to occur right at our very gate. Dad informed the Director that in regard to the banquet, we were going to do what the Bible said and round up all the poor, hungry neighbors and feed them.

Then Dad went out with the mission vehicles and loaded up all the poor people he could find and brought them to our house where he sat them down at the tables with the lace tablecloths and the fine china and we served them the banquet!

I can still remember serving at that banquet when a little old guy, I have never seen before or since, came hobbling up the hill to ask if we could give him a drink of water. He was minus one leg, hobbling around on crutches, had a long white beard and long white hair, looked strange, and wore strange clothes. My dad said, "Sure! In fact we can give you a whole banquet." He took him in and sat him at the head of one of the tables. We gave him a place to stay, and he pronounced a blessing on us before he left the next day. We never saw him again. Even as a kid, I knew that it said somewhere in my Bible that some have entertained angels unawares.

Some of the missionaries became very glad and joyful over what had happened. But others became very hard and bitter and formed a committee to say that my dad should pay for all this personally because the public relations fund was about to go in the red, and how were they going to pay for the real banquet next week when all the invited dignitaries were coming?

The next week the hostile government officials arrived. We showed them around, put on presentations of what we were doing, and fed them another banquet (this time it was pot luck!). Since the PR fund was empty, each missionary family made a dish and sent it over to our house. Miraculously, these men, who had come with their minds already made up to remove our mission from their country went home and decided not to cancel the mission contract after all. God had touched their hearts. I am convinced that the real spiritual battle was won the week before, when we served the first banquet to our poor neighbors.

> *"Then he (Jesus) also said to him that invited him, When thou makest a dinner or a supper, call not thy friends nor thy brethren neither thy kinsmen nor thy rich neighbours, lest they also invite thee again, and a recompense be made thee. But when thou makest a banquet, call the poor, the maimed, the lame, the blind, and thou shalt be blessed ..."* (Luke 14:12-14)

A few weeks later, there was a real move of God among these poor neighbors who lived outside the gate of the mission compound. They formed a little church and got jobs harvesting rice by hand out in the fields, hardly making anything. The rice crop was lost that year, so they did not get any money, and they were starving. Dad decided that whoever came to our door would not be turned away, that if they asked for food, we would share what we had, if they asked for money, we would give each person twenty pesos (equivalent to about five dollars today). We never knew how much money would come in each month, as we were living by faith. We always knew that at the end of the month we would get the bills and the cheque from the mission office, and most of the time they matched. But sometimes we were in the red. Dad gave out more money in that month helping people than we normally received in an entire month. But more needy cases just kept coming, and he would pray about each one and feel that the Lord would lay on his heart to give them so much or to give them something that we had in the house. Some of our fellow missionaries were telling Dad that the people were going to take advantage of him, and he would never be able to stop it; others brought twenty pesos bills of their own over to my parents to help with this endeavor! Dozens of people were helped, and not a one came back to ask for money a second time. When we got our monthly cheque it was for the amount we normally got, plus the sum of all the money that Dad had given away!

Several days later, a woman came to our house and tried to pawn her watch to my mother. She explained that she needed money to buy some presentable clothes for her husband (he only owned torn and stained work clothes), so that she could take him to church (he was too ashamed to go in his work clothes). My mother didn't want to take this poor lady's watch, so she suggested that they pray about the situation. A few minutes later, one of my mom's missionary friends came over with a whole armload of clothes that her son had outgrown. They were the exact size that the lady was looking for, and she was able to take her husband, Miro, to church that very night. He had a glorious encounter with the Lord and a revival was sparked among the poor people.

Then these poor Christians found a sick man

with tuberculosis who was worse off than they were, and they began helping him. No one knew it was tuberculosis but he was very sick and wasted away. My dad got the mission jeep and took the guy to the clinic inside our mission compound. The doctor took one look at him and said, "Chad, you've got to get this guy out of here. He's got tuberculosis. If you leave him here he could infect other people. I don't care what you do, but get rid of him." Dad said, "You mean you're not going to put him in a hospital bed? You're not going to take care of him?" "No! We can't have this infection around! Get him out of here. Take him back where you found him." Dad told him where he found him, and the doctor said, "Don't take him back there either. He'll infect all those people too, and we'll have an epidemic of tuberculosis on our hands. Send him back to his home to die."

Dad pled with the doctor and some of the other missionaries there but no one would budge. As Dad drove away with this sick fellow in the jeep (knowing in his heart that this was not the way the Lord Jesus would have handled this situation), he tried to explain to Miro, the new convert, who did not have anything, the position of the mission, as well as the danger to Miro, his wife and children to be around this guy. Miro said, "We can't do that. If he can't stay in your clinic, he can continue to stay in my home. In fact, I'll give him my bed." They got to Miro's home, and Dad was still saying, "But Miro, you don't understand. This guy has tuberculosis and your home has enough hygiene problems as it is. Show me your bed." Miro's bed was a gunnysack in the corner on the dirt floor of the little hut he lived in. That was what he was going to give this man who was worse off than he was. Miro was going to sleep on the bare ground. As Dad was leaving Miro's house, Miro looked at him and said "My brother died of tuberculosis, and I know exactly what I'm getting into." Miro still seemed a bit confused because what the missionaries were doing did not seem to line up with what he was reading in the Word of God!

My Dad went out and gathered the little congregation of poor believers together, and they all prayed for the sick fellow. Then they took up a collection for him, and there was just enough money to send him to the government TB sanitarium in the state capital. The sick man had a twelve year old son with him, who was well. The two of them were sent down the line on the bus, but half way to the TB hospital, the Lord healed the fellow! He told his son that he knew he was well, but they continued to the sanitarium, where the government doctors took chest x-rays and found no signs of tuberculosis! The next day, they arrived back at our mission compound, and my dad did not even recognize the man (He was in perfect health), until he identified himself!

> *"Is it not to share thy bread with the hungry and that thou bring the poor that are cast out to thy house? when thou seest the naked, that thou cover him; and that thou not hide thyself from thy brother?"* (Isaiah 58:7)

My wife, Marina, is the middle child out of a

more or less typical Colombian family of nine children. We have many relatives. We went through a period of time where it was just one thing after another with her family. We would help one, and then another would be in dire need. One time a business they had went under, and four of them at once were out of work. In Colombia there is no safety net. There is no social security, or unemployment benefits. If the family will not help someone in need, they can literally starve to death. Sometimes it requires great sacrifice.

As the Lord has impressed this verse on us, it has been amazing to look back on the way He has provided. When the four of them were out of work, we prayed. The Lord showed us ways to help three of them, but the only thing that was within our power to do for the fourth was to take our car and trade it for a taxi and have him drive the taxi, support his family and help support my mother-in-law. We had been two years without a car in Colombia and finally the Lord had provided one. I felt in my heart we should do it, as did my wife, but she knew that if we did, we would be without a car, which we needed for the ministry, so it was not an easy choice.

Finally one night I said, "It comes down to this: are we going to help your family or not? If we are, we had better do it." So we did. The answer of the Lord was almost immediate. We turned the car over to the dealer in the morning, and by evening the Lord had provided a car for us that was three times better than the one we gave away. We did not know this would happen when we gave ours away, but the Lord was very good to us.

"Then shall thy light break forth as the morning, and thine health shall spring forth speedily: and thy righteousness shall go before thee ..."

Remember that righteousness also means acts of justice, or doing, as well as being the kind of people God wants us to be. Because we are being the kind of people God wants us to be, we will be doing the kind of things God wants us to do.

"And thy righteousness shall go before thee; the glory of the LORD shall be thy rereward."

We do not even have to defend ourselves from being attacked from behind. God will be watching our backs! The Lord will be protecting us.

"Then shalt thou call, and thou shalt hear the LORD; thou shalt cry, and he shall say, Here I am. If thou take away from the midst of thee the yoke, the putting forth of the finger, and speaking vanity; and if thou pour out thy soul to the hungry, and satisfy the afflicted soul; then shall thy light rise in obscurity, and thy darkenss be as the noonday:" (Isaiah 58:8-10)

If our night is going to become like the noon day, imagine what the noon day will be like? We do not have any idea of the things that God wants to do for us, in us, and through us. **Most of us in our Christian lives use only a fraction of the grace that God has for us**. We never get past making the initial sacrifices involved with giving up our own way. We never get to this part where our light breaks forth like the dawn, our healing quickly appears, our righteousness goes before us, the glory of the Lord becomes our rear guard, and when we call, the Lord answers, "Here am I."

If thou take away from the midst of thee the yoke... This is why it is so important to make sure that we are not one of the ones putting yokes of oppression on other people. We have to make sure that if we need to deal with a problem in someone else's life that it is out of a heart filled with mercy and love. We must not point the finger. But for the grace of God that could be us. We must put ourselves in that person's place and do as we would be done by.

If thou pour out thy soul to the hungry, and satisfy the afflicted soul; then shall thy light rise in obscurity, and thy darkness be as the noonday: and the LORD *shall guide thee continually ..."* sometimes? every once in a while? It says the Lord will guide you **continually**. Can you look at your life and say that the Lord guides you continually? Whenever you cry to the Lord does He say, "Here I am?

and satisfy thy soul in drought, and make fat thy bones; and thou shalt be like a watered garden... If we are truly servants of the Lord, in the middle of a tremendous spiritual conflict raging all around us, then this is not the time for opulence. The Lord has promised to satisfy our needs. Every time He gives us beyond what we need, I believe we should use it for His honor and glory to satisfy the needs of others around us or to see His work go forward as He would lay on our hearts. We need to get back not to our wants, but to our needs. Many times God has blessed me with better things than what I figured I really needed, but that is up to Him. I believe I should look to Him and ask Him for what I need to do the job that He has called me to do. When my needs are being met, I should not come up with another wish list for me, spending money on goodies for me to gratify myself rather than on ammunition to fight the enemy. If you were a soldier in a foxhole, running low on ammunition, what would you want, a load of ice cream or a load of ammunition? Would you rather have a feather bed or what you needed to face the enemy? This is the bottom line. Jesus said:

> *"But seek ye first the kingdom of God and his righteousness, and all these things shall be added unto you."* (Matthew 6:33)

Satan is the "prince of this world" and has most of the worldly resources locked up. Think of what could be done, if even a few of us, were willing to truly release God in our lives through what we have, to be willing to look to Him only for what we need, instead of for what we want. To be willing to ask Him to show us what He wants us to do with our resources. We could begin a dynamic of blessing. God really does want to bless us. There really is prosperity in Jesus Christ, but it is not a selfish prosperity. God wants to prosper us, so that we can reveal God the Father to those in the world who cannot see Him, so that they might see our good works and praise our Father in heaven.

In the Sermon on the Mount, Jesus talks about us being the salt of the earth and the light of the world. We are a city set on a hill that cannot be hidden. Then He says, *Let your light so shine before men that they may see your good works and glorify your Father who is in the heavens.* This is what God is after. We cannot just preach about Jesus Christ and never physically help someone, or the world will not be able to see God the Father. Some churches preach about Christ but never help anyone, and other churches do lots of good works but never tell anyone why. Some churches are preaching and teaching without the anointing of the Holy Spirit to help things go smoothly. God wants everything in its proper place.

I have found that many Christians are victims of a very subtle error (a reordering of truth) that has crept into Christendom and goes something like this: 1) The first step in your Christian life is to accept **Jesus** as your Savior. 2) At a later date in your Christian walk, you may experience a "second work of grace" as **Christ** anoints you with his Holy Spirit (This is referred to by some as "sanctification" and by others as "the baptism in the Holy Spirit". 3) For an elite and special group of saints, there remains an optional third step of making Jesus Christ the **Lord** of their lives. This is normally done only by those who are called into missionary service, into the clergy, or into some type of specialized ministry.

The truth needs to be applied to our practical Christian lives as follows: 1) As the basis of Christian faith, we must receive Jesus Christ who is our Lord and Savior. We must surrender to his authority from the start and renounce our own way (and the ways of the world), so that we might go His way. 2) By grace he will send us the Comfortor

(Holy Spirit) to lead us into all truth and to clothe us (equip us) with the very character and power of God (see 2 Peter Chapter 1). The Holy Spirit will cleanse and purify our hearts so that we might 3) Enter into a right relationship with God the Father.

Only the pure in heart will see God (the Father). It is only through a right relationship with the Father, that we will ever be able to live a victorious Christian life and win the battle against the hosts of darkness. These are the sons of God (the Father) that are joint-heirs with Jesus Christ, and project the peace of the Father into a lost and dying world. These are those who will inspire hope to those who live in darkness.

Look at what will happen:

> "And the LORD shall guide thee continually, and sat-
> isfy thy soul in drought, and make fat thy bones: and
> thou shalt be like a watered garden, and like a spring
> of water, whose waters do not fail." (Isaiah 58:11)

Those around us will have hope and will be able to look at us and will want to be like us. They will want to have what we have; the peace and joy of knowing God. They will want to be able to help others the way we are helping others. They will look at us and say, "Yes, these people are doing what is right. This is real righteousness. This is justice. I wish I could be like that." Jesus wants those in the world to be able to look at our good works (of faith) and praise our Father in heaven, instead of saying, "I don't want to be like that bunch of crazy fanatics over there. Wild horses couldn't drag me into that kooky place." **If we do not present hope to**

the world, and if they cannot see God in us, they will not want to listen to us when we attempt to preach the gospel to them.

Then Isaiah says:

> "And they shall build up out of thee the old waste places: thou shalt raise up the fallen foundations of many generations; and thou shalt be called, The repairer of the breach, The restorer of paths to dwell in." (Isaiah 58:12)

Often what God really wanted is in ruins. The Church started in the upper room, but after a few centuries, it went off into left field. Every now and then a genuine revival would start out in the right direction, yet over the long history of the Church, each one of these moves of God ended up being institutionalized or denominationalized. Men put a yoke where God had meant freedom. They built a cage where God wanted His Holy Spirit to have liberty, and so they kept putting out the fire. God's plans became ancient ruins just like what happened to the children of Israel. But God wants to raise up the fallen foundations, and He wants to build up out of us the old waste places and reconstruct according to His original design.

> "For no one can lay another foundation than that laid, which is Jesus the Christ." (1 Corinthians 3:11)

That which is not built on obedience to Jesus Christ will not stand when the storm comes. Many impressive religious organizations have been built on the sand. If we wish to claim these glorious promises of God from this passage in Isaiah, we must *raise up the fallen foundations*.

> *"And I, if I be lifted up from the earth, will draw all men unto me."* (John 12:32)

Thou shalt be called, The repairer of the breach. The walls around the city were to defend the people from the enemy. Now the spiritual walls of God's protection around our families, our churches, and our society are down and in ruins, so the enemy is coming in like a flood. He is making off with our children; he has wrecked the educational system; he is in the universities, in politics; he runs the economic system. No matter where we turn, it seems that Satan has infiltrated it and is running rampant, because the walls are in ruins. These are spiritual walls that God wanted to have around His people (Church) to protect them. In fact, in a certain sense, God's people, His Church, are supposed to be these spiritual walls of defense that keep the enemy from destroying our society.

If we meet the conditions of this tremendous promise, God says we can rebuild, raise up, repair, and restore what God wanted. We can rebuild the old waste places of the true fortress of God; we can raise up the fallen foundations, raise up the Lord Jesus Christ as the Master of everyone and everything; we can repair the breach and stop the enemy onslaught on God's people; we can restore paths to dwell in, and reconcile our families. The Lord promises in Isaiah 59:19,20 that:

> *"So shall they fear the name of the LORD from the west, and his glory from the rising of the sun; for he*

shall come like a violent river impelled by the breath (or Spirit) of the LORD. And the Redeemer shall come to Zion and unto those that turn from the rebellion in Jacob, said the LORD."

We are getting closer and closer to the time when the Lord Jesus will come back, and every man-made system of hypocrisy, all that has to do with Babylon (confusion), will come down. **We are not talking about renewing man's systems, but about looking to the Lord to redeem his people and deliver them from the bondage that their own "good" ideas have led them into, so that we might build His Kingdom from now on according to His plans instead of our own.**

Thou shalt be called, The repairer of the breach, The restorer of paths to dwell in. One of the things that God wants to restore under His anointing and protection is our families. Families are the basic building block of society and of the Church. The Church will never be strong until it has strong families. Churches as a collection of individuals can only go so far. Satan has attacked the Christian family with all of his might. He has tried to destroy our values, foment sexual perversion, open a "generation gap", promote abortion, and destroy Christian marriage. But before you throw in the towel in the face of this onslaught, listen to the promises of God!

"If thou turn away thy foot from the sabbath, from doing thy will on my holy day; and call the sabbath the delightful, holy, glorious day of the LORD; and shalt honour him by not doing thine own ways, nor

seeking thine own will, nor speaking thine own words:
then shalt thou delight thyself in the LORD; and I will
cause thee to ride upon the high places of the earth
and cause thee to eat of the heritage of Jacob thy fa-
ther: for the mouth of the LORD has spoken it." (Isaiah
58:13-14)

You remember that under the New Covenant,
the Sabbath day, which has to do with God's rest, is
really for us every day. It is every day that God
wants us to rest from being our own god, to rest
from making our own decisions and from striving
to go our own way. He wants us to rest in Him
every day. He still wants us to take at least one day
a week out for physical rest. But for us, every day
should be a Sabbath day. We should enter into and
live in the rest of the Lord, asking Him to lead us,
guide us, fight our battles and go before us. We
need to set our will to follow Him and to do only
those things that He would have us to do.

Let us pray:

Heavenly Father, I ask that You might make us
into overcomers, individually and as a company.
Lord, as we have turned from that which we know
to be wrong in our lives, and as we have gone
over personal relationships that we know need im-
provement, I pray that You would save us from
one of the greatest problems of all. That is from
those things that appear to us to be good, those
things that we think are wonderful, and we are
pleased and complacent with, but there are things
in this category that may really be an abomination before You. Things that we like but that You

do not like. Lord, I pray that You would work in our hearts. Purify our hearts until we can feel the same way that You do about all that is not right in us. So that we will not be deceived by the enemy who would deceive the very elect, if that were possible, into thinking that something is good and of You when that is really not the case.

Lord, I pray for sharp discernment. I ask for Your power and anointing to go forward. I ask that You would take your entire body and form it into a well-trained fighting unit that can go forward to victory, that can reach out to others and help them in Your name, that can stand and shine as a brilliant light that will illuminate the path, so that those outside will be able to find their way to you. That those in the world might see your hope in us and be drawn to open their hearts to You. May everything we do glorify you, Holy Father. Amen.

Chapter

Nine

The Seven Woes

JESUS PUBLIC TEACHING MINISTRY BEGAN WITH THE PROC-
LAMATION OF THE BEATITUDES. It ended with the proclamation of seven woes to the religious leaders of His
day, as they confirmed their rejection of Jesus' message and ministry. After His triumphal entry into
Jerusalem on Palm Sunday, the people were ready
to make Jesus their king, until He entered the temple
and began driving out the buyers and sellers. His
decision to cleanse the temple for the second time
by overturning the tables of the moneychangers
precipitated a conflict with the chief priests, scribes,
Pharisees, and other leaders. If Jesus were truly
going to be King, then he would have to dismantle
all the corrupt religious machinery that was standing between the people and a right relationship with
God. The din and chaos of the buyers and sellers
was drowning out true communication with God.

"and (he) *said unto them, It is written, My house shall be called the house of prayer; but ye have made it a den of thieves."* (Matthew 21:13)

The people wanted Jesus as their King as long as He just confined His ministry to the working of miracles. They wanted to be fed and healed, but they did not want radical surgery to their religious way of life. There were many who felt carnally secure in their ability to procure the proper offering or sacrifice with money at their own convenience. These were the buyers that Jesus drove from the temple. The sellers, represented by the religious leaders, were even more dependent on this illicit economic activity in the House of God, because it was their prime source of income. When Jesus interrupted their flow of cash right at passover (the most profitable time of the year), they reacted desperately.

After several pointed parables by the Lord, these evil men tried to trap Jesus by asking Him difficult questions. They failed miserably, and the scripture says:

"And no one was able to answer him a word, neither dared anyone from that day forth ask him any more questions.

Then Jesus spoke to the multitude and to his disciples, saying, The scribes and the Pharisees have sat down in Moses' seat; therefore, whatever they bid you to observe, observe it and do it, but do not act according to their works, for they say and do not do it.

For they bind burdens that are heavy and grievous to

bear and lay them on men's shoulders, but they them-
selves will not move them with one of their fingers.
But they do all their works that they may be seen of
men: they make broad their phylacteries and enlarge
the borders of their garments and love the first place
at feasts and the chief seats in the synagogues and
greetings in the markets and to be called of men, Rabbi,
Rabbi.

But, as for you, desire not to be called Rabbi, for one
is your Master, the Christ; and you are all brothers.
And call no one your father upon the earth, for one is
your Father, who is in the heavens. Neither be ye
called masters, for one is your Master, the Christ. But
he that is the greatest among you shall be your ser-
vant. And whosoever shall exalt himself shall be
humbled, and he that shall humble himself shall be
exalted." (Matthew 22:46 - 23:12)

Jesus then proclaimed the seven woes, which correlate perfectly with the seven Beatitudes in Matthew, chapter five. With the proclamation of these woes, Jesus makes it clear that not only did the scribes and Pharisees reject Him and His message; they insisted on doing the exact opposite! Let us study these woes, one by one and contrast them with the Beatitudes.

The first woe:

"But woe unto you, scribes and Pharisees, hypocrites!
*for **ye shut up the kingdom of the heavens in**
__front of men__; for ye neither go in yourselves, nei-
ther suffer ye those that are entering to go in." (Matthew 23:13)

The first Beatitude:

*"Blessed are the poor in spirit, for **theirs is the kingdom of the heavens.**"*

Not only do these proud religious leaders refuse to enter the true Kingdom of Heaven, they stand in the way and prevent others from entering in. When those outside observe these "representatives" of God, they see nothing but hypocrisy, avarice, and greed; causing many to reject the Gospel. The church age is going to close with a time of extreme woe for those church leaders who refuse to enter the Kingdom of God through the narrow gate and at the same time prevent others from doing so; those who have only made a shallow, superficial commitment to God and teach others to do the same. **God cannot judge the world until He cleans up His church first!** Given the degree of selfishness and corruption rampant in the church today, many of those in the world can't really be blamed for rejecting it.

The second woe:

"Woe unto you, scribes and Pharisees, hypocrites! for ye compass sea and land to make one proselyte, and when he is made, ye make him twofold more a son of hell than yourselves." (Matthew 23:15)

The second Beatitude:

"Blessed are those that mourn, for they shall be comforted."

Those who have truly chosen to follow Christ have to leave many things that are dear to them behind as they take up their cross and follow Him. "Only he who loses his life for my sake and the Gospel will find it", says the Lord. The one who is dead in Christ will also experience the resurrection power of God that raised Jesus from the dead: He will be comforted, that is he will receive the Comforter. The Comforter is nothing less than God's Holy Spirit. Those who have the Holy Spirit, are sealed by God, and operate in His authority. Those who mourn are sincere with God. They are not hypocrites.

The comforted follow only the still small voice of Jesus Christ, and they win converts that follow Jesus Christ. The "scribes and Pharisees" on the other hand, win proselytes to their sect, order, or denomination. The comforted pay attention to the ways of the Lord and realize (like Moses) that how we implement the Kingdom of God (our modus operandi) is many times more important than our plans and ambitions. The proselytes of the scribes and Pharisees of religious humanism believe that the end justifies the means. They think nothing of taking the law into their own hands to implement their lofty plans and ambitions by using God's name.

The third woe:

"Woe unto you, ye blind guides, who say, Whosoever shall swear by the temple, it is nothing; but whosoever shall swear by the gold of the temple, he is a debtor! Ye fools and blind, for which is greater, the gold or the temple that sanctifies the gold? And, Whosoever shall swear by the altar, it is nothing; but who-

soever swears by the gift that is upon it, he is a debtor.
Ye fools and blind, for which one is greater, the gift or
the altar that sanctifies the gift? Whosoever therefore
shall swear by the altar, swears by it and by all things
thereon. And whosoever shall swear by the temple,
swears by it and by Him that dwells therein. And he
that shall swear by the heaven, swears by the throne
of God and by Him that sits thereon." (Matthew 23:16-
22)

The third Beatitude:

"Blessed are the meek, for they shall inherit the earth."

The meek are those who submit every area of
their existence to the Lordship of Jesus Christ.
The hypocrite will do the opposite; he will interpret God's precepts according to his own understanding, or according to the doctrine of his organization.

The scribes and Pharisees, as opposed to the
meek, are busy trying to save their lives and their
worldly treasures. Since they do not have the genuine Holy Spirit, they lack the authority of God in
their dealings with others. This is why they invoke
oaths. They will swear by the gold of the temple,
but an oath by the temple is nothing to them; by
the gift on the altar, but an oath by the altar is non-
binding. They cannot bear to pay the cost of putting their all on the altar and actually becoming
part of that great temple made without hands that
God is raising up as His dwelling place.

In the Sermon on the Mount, Jesus tells us to
not swear oaths by anything. We are to let our yes
be yes and our no be no. Jesus says that anything

beyond this comes of evil. Jesus Christ must have complete authority over us if we are to be able to speak with His authority. Those unwilling to mourn over their own plans will never receive the Holy Spirit. Without the real Holy Spirit they will never be able to be meek before the Lord . They will never speak with true authority from God. Therefore they will fall into the trap of the devil and justify their actions with pious sounding oaths. At present no one can swear an oath by the gold of the temple or by the gift on the altar because all of that was destroyed precisely as a result of the fulfillment of Jesus' prophetic words of authority in this section of Scripture. It has been my experience in North America to hear many swear by the Bible and in South America to hear many swear by their mother (or by Jesus' mother) when they do not have true authority from God.

The meek are those who moved by the Spirit of God place all aspects of their existence under the Authority of Jesus Christ. The blind guides do exactly the opposite, they interpret the precepts of God according to their own criteria or according to the doctrine of their religious confession.

The fourth woe:

*"Woe unto you, scribes and Pharisees, hypocrites! for ye pay tithe of mint and anise and cummin and have omitted that which is more important of the law: **judgment, mercy,** and **faith**; these were expedient for ye to have done, and not to leave the other undone. Ye blind guides, who strain at a gnat and swallow a camel."* (Matthew 23:23,24)

The fourth Beatitude:

*"Blessed are those who hunger and thirst for **righteousness,** for they shall be satisfied."*

Righteousness is the manifestation of right judgment and mercy and faith in our lives that occurs only when God's Holy Spirit dwells within us. Righteousness is composed of these two components: 1) Being (through grace) the person God wants us to be and 2) Doing (by faith) those acts of justice and mercy that God wants us to do. It is both being and doing right. This is what the religious legalists are never able to obtain no matter how hard they try. They are always striving hard to tithe the mint, dill, and cummin (the smallest herbs in the garden), while they neglect the foundational virtues of the Christian faith. **Being filled with the presence of God is the only way to rest and be satisfied.** The legalist will never be satisfied, no matter how many "good" rules he tries to keep, or how many "excellent" Christian principles he tries to implement in his own strength.

The fifth woe:

*"Woe unto you, scribes and Pharisees, hypocrites! for ye make clean the outside of the cup or of the platter, but within they are full of **extortion** and **incontinence**. Thou blind Pharisee, cleanse first that which is within the cup and platter that the outside of them may be clean also."* (Matthew 23:25,26)

The fifth Beatitude:

*"Blessed are the **merciful**, for they shall obtain mercy."*

Showing mercy means treating others the way we would like to be treated ourselves. It is being willing to forgive and restore our brother (or even our enemy) who has wronged us. It is the sacrificial love of God flowing from a tender heart filled with compassion for those in need. Extortion and incontinence are the exact opposite of mercy. They take advantage of those in need. The religious hypocrite has an outwardly pious appearance but is always ready to pounce on and devour others whenever it is to his advantage to do so. **There are many "charitable" ministries that actually live off of the predicament of the poor people they are claiming to help.**

The sixth woe:

"Woe unto you, scribes and Pharisees, hypocrites! for ye are like unto whitewashed sepulchres, who indeed appear beautiful outside, but inside are full of dead men's bones and of all uncleanness. Even so ye also outwardly appear righteous unto men, but within ye are full of hypocrisy and iniquity." (Matthew 23:27,28)

The sixth Beatitude:

"Blessed are the pure in heart, for they shall see God."

It takes a pure heart to see God. The heart is the mirror of our soul, created to reflect the image of God. If it is stained and defiled with hypocrisy and iniquity it will never reflect the image of God. This is what causes spiritual blindness. The reason that Jesus has been calling these seemingly respectable religious leaders "blind guides" is because their hearts are rotten to the core. Jesus says that if the blind lead the blind, both will fall into a pit. (see Luke 6:39)

The seventh woe:

"Woe unto you, scribes and Pharisees, hypocrites! because ye build the tombs of the prophets and adorn the sepulchres of the righteous and say, If we had been in the days of our fathers, we would not have been partakers with them in the blood of the prophets. Therefore ye are witnesses unto yourselves that ye are the **sons of those who murdered the prophets***. Fill ye up then the measure of your fathers. Ye serpents, ye generation of vipers, how can ye escape the judgment of hell?"* (Matthew 23:29-33)

The seventh Beatitude:

"Blessed are the peacemakers, for they shall be called the **sons of God***."*

Here we have the true "sons of God" on one hand and those who witness against themselves that they are the "sons of those who murdered the prophets" on the other. The pure hearts of the sons of God radiate peace (integrity). The rotten hearts of the hypocrites (which are full of extortion and incontinence) generate murder and violence towards those who would attempt to illuminate them with God's truth. (Bear in mind that Jesus equates harboring an angry grudge with murder in Matthew 5:21)

"Therefore, behold, I send unto you prophets and wise men and scribes, and some of them ye shall kill and crucify, and some of them ye shall scourge in your synagogues and persecute them from city to city, that upon you may come all the righteous blood shed upon

the earth from the blood of righteous Abel unto the blood of Zacharias son of Barachias, whom ye murdered between the temple and the altar. Verily I say unto you, All these things shall come upon this generation.

O Jerusalem, Jerusalem, thou that didst kill the prophets and stone those who are sent unto thee, how often I desired to gather thy children together, even as a hen gathers her chickens under her wings, and ye would not! Behold, your house is left unto you desolate. For I say unto you, Ye shall not see me from now on until ye shall say, Blessed is he that comes in the name of the Lord." (Matthew 23:34-39)

Compare the above Scripture to the continuation of the remaining two Beatitudes in Matthew Chapter five.

"Blessed are those who suffer persecution for righteousness' sake, for theirs is the kingdom of the heavens.

Blessed are ye when men shall revile you and persecute you and shall say all manner of evil against you falsely for my sake. Rejoice and be exceeding glad, for great is your reward in the heavens; for so they persecuted the prophets who were before you." (Matthew 5:10,11)

For the sons of God, persecution is the mark of true sonship. But woe to those who are doing the persecution. The hypocrites will always persecute the true sons of God. The religious traditions of men will always contradict the true revelation of God. Prophets do not normally get into serious trouble until they try to drive the buyers and sellers from the temple. When the "buyers" are told that they may bypass the temple vendors and go directly to God the Father with their problems and concerns through the mediation of the Lord Jesus Christ; when the "sellers" are confronted for building their own kingdoms in the name of the Lord, for using the things of God to line their own pockets and exalt their own name (or the name of their organization) instead of God's name; when the existing religious machinery becomes threatened by the prophetic Word of the Lord; then watch out: This is when the "generation of vipers" will attack. They will attack whenever they are cornered and their kingdom is threatened. It has been said that: *Those who attempt to do God's work man's way will always persecute those who do God's work God's way.*

> *"And Jesus went out and departed from the temple, and his disciples came to him to show him the buildings of the temple. And Jesus said unto them, See ye not all these things? verily I say unto you, There shall not be left here one stone upon another that shall not be thrown down."* (Matthew 24:1,2)

The Old Testament age ended with the complete destruction of the temple about 70 AD. After the temple had been burned, Roman soldiers pried apart every stone seeking precious metals that had melted in the fire and had trickled down into the cracks. All of the apostate religious machinery that rejected the Lord was completely destroyed. Not one stone was left on top of another. Not one ounce of the temple gold that the Pharisees had sworn their oaths by was left. Even though almost everyone and everything in Jerusalem was destroyed, all the true Christians escaped unharmed. In the confusion surrounding the Roman siege of Jerusalem, two opposing factions of Jews had a bloody fight for control of the temple citadel. The Christians took this as the sign given by the Lord and fled (the abomination of desolation spoken of by the prophet Daniel).

We are now drawing nearer and nearer to the end of the Church Age (the New Testament Age). Jesus is still saying **Blessed, Blessed, Blessed** to those who come to him as poor in spirit, to receive forgiveness for their sins and proclaim Him Lord of their lives. But he is saying **woe! woe! woe!** to those who stand in the way of those who would enter the narrow gate that leads to life. He is saying **woe! woe! woe!** to those self-righteous hypocrites who are still doing the exact opposite of His Gospel as set forth in the Beatitudes. He is saying **woe! woe! woe!** to those who continue to persecute His prophets in order to save their man-made kingdoms and traditions.

Make no mistake. Before the end of this age, God will make as thorough an end to the present man-ordained religious machinery as He did in the last age. Only those houses that are truly founded on the rock will stand when the rains come down and the floods rise and the wind beats upon the structures that we have built in the name of the Lord.

"See that you do not refuse him that speaks. For if those who refused him that spoke on earth did not

escape, much less shall we escape, if we turn away from him that speaks from the heavens, whose voice then shook the earth; but now he has promised, saying, Yet even once, I shall shake not the earth only, but also the heaven. And this word, Yet even once, signifies the removing of those things that are shaken, as of things that are made, that those things which cannot be shaken may remain.

Therefore, receiving a kingdom which cannot be moved, let us hold fast to the grace, by which we serve God, pleasing him with reverence and godly fear: for our God is a consuming fire." (Hebrews 12:25-29)

Overcoming the Curse

*"Blessed is he that reads and those that hear the words
of this prophecy and keep those things which are written therein, for the time is at hand."* (Revelation 1:3)

DID YOU KNOW THAT THERE ARE SEVEN BEATITUDES scat-
tered throughout the book of Revelation? Amaz-
ingly there is a perfect correlation between them
and the Beatitudes of Matthew Chapter 5. I would
like to close this book by comparing them for you
in the light of the Lord's Prayer (which also has seven
parts).

The Beatitudes are the synthesis of the Gospel
message preached by Jesus Christ. The Lord's Prayer
is the response from our hearts that Jesus desires
when we hear and receive His message. The Beatitudes of Revelation are a further amplification of
the full ramifications of this message. Revelation
gives us insight into how God's Plan for Battle is

implemented in the unseen spiritual world and how that in turn impacts the material world that we perceive with our five senses.

Recent world events have triggered a flurry of Christian literature on the book of Revelation. Along with greatly increased interest in end time events it is also evident that many believers fear the cataclysmic judgements described in the Apocalypse of John. ***Too many paranoid "Christians" spend their time trying to side-step the effects of the curse rather than laying hold of the Blessings of God by faith.*** The gist of many commentators' interpretations of this book seem to center on complicated theological explanations of how only those who adhere to their doctrine, or school of thought will be spared from or preserved during "the great tribulation" and exempted from the "great white throne judgement". Since most of these "explanations" are at odds with one another, the overall effect of this controversy has been to submit the body of Christ to an intense form of intellectual terrorism. We forget that:

> *"...God is charity, and he that abides in charity abides in God, and God in him. In this the charity with us is made perfect, that we may have confidence in the day of judgment, that as he is, so are we in this world. In charity there is no fear; but charity that is perfect casts out fear; because fear has torment; from which he that fears is not complete in charity. We love him, because he first loved us."* (1 John 4:16-19)

There is a base cause underneath all of the vicious controversy surrounding the interpretation of end time events. ***Those whose security is in their doctrines will desperately attack anyone who attempts to present a conflicting view.*** We must remember that our doctrines cannot save us (even if they are true). In the last chapter we saw that right doctrine alone could not and did not save the scribes and Pharisees. A right relationship with the Lord Jesus Christ (which in turn will bring us into a proper relationship with our "brother") is our only hope.

> *"We love him, because he first loved us. If anyone says, I love God and hates his brother, he is a liar; for he that does not love his brother whom he has seen, how can he love God whom he has not seen? And we have this commandment from him, That he who loves God loves his brother also."* (1 John 4:19-21)

Jesus Christ is not a terrorist. He is called Faithful and True and with justice He judges and makes war (see Rev. 19:11). ***Those who allow their fears of the future to dictate their eschatology could miss the still small voice of the Lord as He calls everyone to follow Him to the only true place of protection.*** He Himself is our ark of safety and He longs to gather us up as a mother hen shelters her chicks under her wings (see Matthew 23:37). Will we let Him? Or will we continue to insist on our own man-made doctrines of security. For those who are sheltered in Christ, the seven Beatitudes of Revelation promise hope, rest, protection, eternal satisfaction, freedom from fear, victory over evil, and power and authority in the tree of life! Let us set aside our preconceived fears

regarding this book and discover the great and glorious promises of God.

The first Beatitude:

*"Blessed are **the poor in spirit**, for theirs is the kingdom of the heavens."*

The first line of the Lord's Prayer:

*"Our Father, who art in the heavens, **Hallowed be
thy name**."*

The first Beatitude of Revelation:

*"Blessed is he that **reads** and those that **hear** the
words of this prophecy, and **keep** those things which
are written therein, for the time is at hand."* (Revelation 1:3)

We have seen that the only way into the Kingdom of Heaven is through the narrow gate. We
must choose to be poor in spirit and allow God to
deal with our pride. We must repent of going our
own way and receive forgiveness for our sins. Our
own righteousness is as filthy rags before God. It is
His Name and His way that must be hallowed and
exalted, not ours. The path to God's blessing begins when we **read**, **hear**, and then **keep** the Revelation of Jesus Christ. A mental knowledge of God
is not enough. We must take His Revelation to heart
if we are to obtain His blessing. Do you have a
heart knowledge of Jesus Christ, or only a head
knowledge?

The second Beatitude:

*"Blessed are those that mourn, for they shall be com-
forted."*

The second line in the Lord's Prayer:

"Thy kingdom come,"

The second Beatitude in Revelation:

"And I heard a voice from heaven saying unto me, Write, Blessed are the dead who die in the Lord from now on; Yea, saith the Spirit, that they may rest from their labours, and their works do follow them." (Revelation 14:13)

This Beatitude does not just refer to those who have physically died knowing the Lord, it is of supreme importance to those of us still alive. It is the key to obtaining the victory.

"For we are buried with him by baptism into death, that just as the Christ was raised up from the dead to the glory of the Father, likewise we also walk in newness of life. For if we have been planted together in him in the likeness of his death, we shall be also in the likeness of his resurrection, knowing this: that our old man is crucified with him that the body of sin might be destroyed that we should not serve sin any longer." (Romans 6:4-6)

"For the charity of the Christ constrains us because we judge thus: that if one died for all, then all are dead: And that he died for all that those who live should not live from now on unto themselves, but unto him who died and rose again for them." (2 Corinthians 5:14,15)

A lot of water has gone under the bridge between the first and second Beatitudes of Revelation. Let me give you a brief summary of these fourteen chapters. *A glorious, radiant, all-powerful Jesus Christ has been revealed.* His bosom friend, John, took one look at him and fell at Jesus' feet as though dead! This is what we must do as well if we are to receive and transmit to others the revelation of the power, authority, and victory of the risen Savior who holds the keys of death and Hades.

Christ immediately dictates seven letters to John. These letters are addressed to seven specific churches who represent the Church at large. The letters are filled with encouragement and exhortation but sin and apostasy in the Church will be judged. Loss of the "first love", "lukewarmness" and hypocrisy will not be tolerated. Those participating in the "practices of the Nicotaitans", those who are of the "synagogue of Satan", those who hold to the "teaching of Baalam", those who "tolerate that woman Jezebel", those who have "soiled their clothes", ignored God's Word and denied His Name will be dealt with directly by Christ. *For it is time that judgment begins from the House of the Lord!* (1 Peter 4:17)

Those who overcome in the Name of the Lord are promised: The right to eat of the "tree of life"; they will not be hurt by the "second death"; they will be given "hidden manna' and a "new name"; they will be given authority over the nations and the "morning star"; they are to be dressed in white, their names will never be erased from the "book of life", and Jesus will acknowledge them before His Father and His Father's angels; they will become pillars in the temple of God with the Name of God, the Name of the new Jerusalem, and Christs' new name written on them; plus they will have the right to sit with Jesus Christ on His throne as Christ sits with His Father on the Father's throne!

Next comes the glorious revelation of God the Father's throne in heaven. Jesus mission to "planet earth" was to rescue and redeem creation, bringing everything back into a right relationship with God the Father. In the fall, Adam had signed the "title deed" of the first creation over to Satan. It was sealed with seven "seals" and no one was found worthy to open them, causing great sorrow to John. Through the victory of His death on the cross, the "lamb that was slain" was found worthy to open the seals and the legal title of creation was restored back to its rightful owner.

The Old Testament concept of redemption was this: If a man sold his land to another (leaving his children without inheritance) his relative, or kinsman could "pay the price" and redeem the property (Leviticus 25:23-28). The mortgage was drawn up on a scroll with the specfications of the land on one side and the signatures on the other side. Then it was sealed. When the "kinsman redeemer" (such as Boaz in the Book of Ruth) payed off the mortgage, the seals were broken and the legal title returned to its proper owner. In the case of this earth, however, even though Jesus Christ regained legal title at the cross, Satan, the lawless one, refuses to leave and must be evicted.

As Jesus Christ opens the seals one by one and begins the process of redemption a great spiritual battle is joined against the kingdom of darkness. God's saints begin to carry out His **Plan for Battle**. The Gospel of the Kingdom is to be preached to all nations and the earth is to be "harvested" before the end comes. **Those who voluntarily receive the Lord Jesus Christ will ultimately be separated from those who do not.** Those who are faithful with little will be given greater responsibility in the age to come.

As the battle rages, God places His "seal" on the foreheads of all those who are His. God's seal is the Holy Spirit (see Ephesians 1:13). Satan also places a "mark" on the hands and foreheads of those who worship him. Those who bear Satan's mark act and think like he does. They prefer going their own way. They do not obey God. Instead they persecute those who wear God's "mark". But nothing can touch those who are "dead in Christ" and sealed by the Holy Spirit. Even if they face physical martyrdom, they arrive unharmed to the throne of God to rule and reign with Christ! Soon there is a great multitude that no man can number from every nation, tribe, people, and language standing before the throne in white robes waving palm branches in their hands.

When the seventh seal of the legal title to creation is opened, Jesus Christ, the the rightful owner, is now ready to evict Satan, his hosts of darkness, and all their followers. Now, in response to the prayers of "all the saints", the trumpets begin to sound. The trumpets announce the message: **The people of God must set aside their man-**

made kingdoms and differences of opinion to rally together under the banner of the Lordship and authority of Jesus Christ for the final battle. The children of Israel blew seven trumpets and marched around the walls of Jericho until God brought the enemy walls down. *The trumpets rally the people of God, proclaim the rightful ownership and authority of Christ over everyone and everything, and strike fear and terror into the hearts of the enemy.*

As the time draws near for the seventh and last trumpet to sound, a powerful "angel" that coincides perfectly with the glorious description of Jesus Christ in Revelation chapter one, descends to earth from heaven with an open "scroll" (title deed to the earth) in His hand. He places His right foot on the sea (the world), and His left foot on the land (the church) (see Psalm 95:5) and takes legal possession of the earth with a *"roar like a lion"*. Note that Jesus begins his work of redemption as a "Lamb that was slain" but he returns to claim His possesion and evict the enemy with a "roar like a lion". The Lamb of God is also the Lion of Judah. Seven Thunders sound and He proclaims that there will be no more delay. Soon the seventh trumpet sounds, and

> *"The kingdoms of this world are reduced unto our Lord and to his Christ; and he shall reign for ever and ever."*
> (Revelation 11:15)

John is also given revelation from other perspectives such as "measuring the temple of God and the altar". John is allowed to witness the "war in heaven" as the dragon (Satan) and his angels are driven from heaven by Michael and the heavenly hosts. The "dragon" and his followers are hurled to earth and lose no time making war against the saints as they dominate the "world" through a many headed system of control involving secular power, economic might and false religion.

The dragon's kingdom runs on fear, terror, greed, and avarice. It will ultimately collapse because "A kingdom divided against itself cannot stand" (see Matthew 12:25,26) The many headed beast, the false prophet, and the great harlot can dominate the world, but they will continually war among themselves. They all want to go their own way and feed their own selfishness and pride. The only way poor Satan can hold his shaky empire together is by force.

> "... those that worship the beast and its image and who-soever receives the mark of its name, have no rest day or night." (Revelation 14:11)

If we have truly turned from our own way and set our will to follow the Lord Jesus Christ, we must renounce the many worldly pursuits that used to give us monetary income, power, prestige, or plea-sure. The Apostle James says that friendship with the world is enmity with God. If we renounce the world to follow Jesus Christ, we will be comforted. God will send us the Comforter, His Holy Spirit. It is only by the power and anointing of the Holy Spirit within us that we can ever hope to do the will of God here on earth as it is done in heaven.

After we have been emptied of ourselves, God

wants to purify us and fill us with himself. He is to be our righteousness. We are to be clothed in white garments as we do His will. His Spirit is the **Holy** Spirit. After we have been divested of our pride in our own righteousness, which is as filthy rags before God (see Isaiah 64:6), He will cleanse us from the inside out and cover us with Jesus' righteousness. He will clothe us with His Spirit.

When Jesus comes back, everyone will be exposed for what they are. If we have truly died to ourselves and been crucified with Christ, then we are dead to sin, and alive through the resurrection power of the Holy Spirit to live for Jesus Christ. Those who are not clothed with the genuine Holy Spirit of Christ will be shamefully exposed when He unexpectedly returns.

> *"And when the king came in to see the guests, he saw there a man who did not have on a wedding garment, and he said unto him, Friend, how didst thou come in here not having a wedding garment? And he was speechless.*
>
> *Then the king said to the servants, Bind him hand and foot and take him away and cast him into the darkness outside; there shall be weeping and gnashing of teeth. For many are called, but few are chosen."* (Matthew 22:11-14)

The system of this world is going to be destroyed. Everything that can be shaken will be shaken. Revelation speaks of seven "vials" of the wrath of God that will be poured out to cleanse the earth and bring about the destruction of the "beast" and his kingdom. But **what is dark-**

ness and gloom for the children of darkness will be gladness and light for those clothed with the Spirit of God (Joel 3:12-16). When the land of Egypt was devastated by the ten plagues, the land of Goshen (where God's people lived) was unscathed.

> *"For, behold, the day comes that shall burn as an oven; and all the proud, and all that do wickedly shall be stubble; and the day that comes shall burn them up, said the LORD of the hosts, that it shall leave them neither root nor branch.*
>
> *But unto you that fear my name shall the Sun of righteousness be born, and in his wings he shall bring saving health; and ye shall go forth and jump like calves of the herd. And ye shall tread down the wicked; for they shall be ashes under the soles of your feet in the day that I make, said the LORD of the hosts."* (Malachi 4:1-3)

Right now, near the end of the Church Age, we are in the time of the harvest. The fields are white unto harvest and the will of the Lord is to send out laborers to reap the precious harvest of souls before the end comes. It is imperative that we be clothed with the Spirit of God so that we might inspire hope to a world that is lost and dying. The world is tired of listening to the hypocrites representing man-made religion. Those who our Lord referred to as "whitewashed tombs, which outwardly appear beautiful, but within are full of dead men's bones and all uncleanness" have been unable to keep the gates of Hades from prevailing against their "churches". But the Lord is raising up a band of overcomers, clothed in His righteousness and led by His Spirit; they will prevail against the forces of darkness.

The third Beatitude:

"Blessed are the meek, for they shall inherit the earth."

The third line of the Lords Prayer:

"Thy will be done in earth as it is in heaven."

The third Beatitude from Revelation:

"Behold, I come as a thief. Blessed is he that watches and keeps his garments lest he walk naked, and they see his shame. (Revelation 16:15)

The meek are those who submit to the Master. They are like the horse who can be counted on to willingly obey his master, even in the heat of battle. The goal of the meek is to see their Master's kingdom come. This is how they will inherit the earth. But in order to be victorious, the meek must die to their own way. They must place everything, even their best ideas, possessions, gifts, and abilities on the altar and "rest from their (own) labor". Then their "deeds (of victorious faith) will follow them". This is what it means to be clothed in fine linen (see Revelation 19:7,8).

The fourth Beatitude:

"Blessed are those who hunger and thirst for righteousness, for they shall be satisfied."

The fourth line of the Lord's Prayer:

"Give us this day our daily bread."

The fourth beatitude of Revelation:

*"And he said unto me, Write, Blessed are those who are called unto the marriage supper of the Lamb. And he said unto me, **These are the true words of God.**"* (Revelation 19:9)

Those who are born of God's Spirit, that are born again, find that they have different desires and appetites than they had before. They hunger and thirst to please God, who promises to fill them with Himself. This is symbolised by the Lord's supper and speaks of the New Covenant, which is Christ in you, the hope of glory.

The Lord's prayer mentions our daily bread, and the Scripture says that *Man shall not live by bread alone, but by every word that proceeds out of the mouth of God.* Jesus said that, *I AM the living bread which came down from heaven; if anyone eats of this bread they shall live for ever.* In another place He said that, *Unless ye eat the flesh of the Son of man and drink his blood, ye shall have no life in you.*

Those who are invited to the "wedding supper of the Lamb" will be filled and satisfied in the presence of the Lord for all eternity! They will feed exclusively on *the true words of God.* Revelation features two women: Christ will return for a bride "without spot or wrinkle". On the other hand, Babylon the Great, mother of prostitutes and of all the abominations of the earth, will be completely destroyed. Abominations are totally incompatible with the presence of God. The one will exclude the other. **The imminent return of Christ precipitates a cataclysmic end on "mystery Babylon". God's people are called to "come out of her," lest we share in her destruction.**

Upon the destruction of Babylon, there is great joy in heaven. But it is a double celebration. **The celebration of the destruction of Babylon is also the celebration of the wedding supper of the Lamb.**

A great multitude in heaven shouts:

"And again they said, Halelu-JAH. And her smoke rose up for ever and ever. And the twenty-four elders and the four animals fell upon their faces and worshipped God that was seated upon the throne, saying, Amen! Halelu-JAH!

And a voice came out of the throne, saying, Praise our God, all ye his servants and ye that fear him, both small and great. And I heard as it were the voice of a great company and as the voice of many waters and as the voice of mighty thunderings, saying, Halelu-JAH; for the Lord God almighty reigns.

Let us be glad and rejoice and give glory to him; for the marriage of the Lamb is come, and his bride has made herself ready. And to her was granted that she should be arrayed in fine linen, clean and bright: for the fine linen is the righteousness of the saints." (Revelation 19:3-8)

I find a great similarity between this Scripture and the parable of the wheat and the tares.

"He put forth another parable unto them, saying, The kingdom of the heavens is likened unto a man who sows good seed in his field but while men slept, his enemy came and sowed tares among the wheat and went away. But when the blade was sprung up and brought forth fruit, then the tares appeared also.

So the servants of the husband of the house came and said unto him, Lord, didst thou not sow good seed in thy field? from where then does it have tares? He said unto them, The enemy, a man, has done this. The servants said unto him, Wilt thou then that we go and gather them up?

But he said, No, lest while ye gather up the tares, ye root up also the wheat with them. Let both grow together until the harvest, and in the time of harvest I will say to the reapers, Gather ye together **first the tares** *and bind them in bundles to burn them, but gather the wheat into my barn."* (Matthew 13:24-30)

Jesus himself was the seed that fell into the ground and died so that it might bear fruit in great abundance. His wheat, or church, has been mixed with tares from the beginning of this Church age. Notice, however, that at harvest time, he is going to **gather and burn the tares first** and then gather the wheat into His barn.

Listen to Jesus' explanation of this parable:

"He answered and said unto them, He that sows the good seed is the Son of man; the field is the world; the good seed are the sons of the kingdom, but the tares are the sons of the wicked; and the enemy that sowed them is the devil; the harvest is the end of the age, and the reapers are the angels.

As therefore the tares are gathered and burned in the fire, so shall it be in the end of this age. The Son of man shall send forth his angels, and they shall gather out of his kingdom all things that offend and those who do iniquity and shall cast them into the furnace of fire; there shall be wailing and gnashing of teeth. Then shall the righteous shine forth as the sun in the kingdom of their Father. He who has ears to hear, let him hear." (Matthew 13:37-43)

God is getting ready to clean house. He is going to uproot and remove all that causes sin and all who do evil from His Kingdom (Church). The destruction of Babylon will leave His Church without spot or wrinkle, ready for the wedding supper of the Lamb.

The fifth Beatitude:

"Blessed are the merciful, for they shall obtain mercy."

The fifth line of the Lord's Prayer:

"And set us free from our debts, as we set free our debtors."

The fifth Beatitude in Revelation:

"Blessed and holy is he that has part in the first resurrection; on such the second death has no authority, but they shall be priests of God and of the Christ and shall reign with him a thousand years." (Revelation 20:6)

Those whom Christ invites to share his throne will be tender channels of His love and mercy. They will heal the brokenhearted, proclaim liberty to the captives, and open the prison doors to those who are bound. They will not take advantage of anyone. No one with a root of bitterness or who is interested in exacting revenge will be "a priest of God" and "reign with Christ". Jesus personifies mercy, while at the same time He is just, faithful, and true. After He cleanses His Church, in His mercy, Jesus will judge the world. The most merciful thing He can do, is rid the world of the selfishness, rebellion, and pride that are causing so much pain and sorrow. True mercy is faithful to insist on justice for those unable or unwilling to take the law into their own hands and defend themselves. Now Jesus will cleanse the world of those who are filled with extorsion and incontinence. He will turn the tables and now some of the last shall be first and some of those who were first shall be last.

> "And I saw the heaven open, and behold a white horse; and he that was seated upon him was called Faithful and True, and in righteousness he judges and makes war. And his eyes were as a flame of fire, and on his head were many crowns; and he had a name written, that no one has known, but he himself. And he was clothed with a garment dipped in blood; and his name is called The Word of God.
>
> And the armies that are in the heaven followed him upon white horses, clothed in fine linen, white and clean. And out of his mouth goes a sharp sword, that with it he should smite the Gentiles; and he shall rule them with a rod of iron; and he treads the winepress of the fierceness and wrath of Almighty God. And he has on his garment and on his thigh a name written, KING OF KINGS, AND LORD OF LORDS." (Revelation 19:11-16)

The sixth Beatitude:

"Blessed are the pure in heart, for they shall see God."

The sixth line in the Lord's Prayer:

"And lead us not into temptation, but deliver us from evil,"

The sixth Beatitude in Revelation:

"Behold, I come quickly; blessed is he that keeps the words of the prophecy of this book." (Revelation 22:7)

The pure in heart are full of integrity. They are empty of themselves and overflowing with the Holy Spirit. Springs of living water flow from their soul. They project God's peace. They are the only ones who will be able to "keep the words of the prophecy of this book". (The word for "book" here, *Biblion* is the root for our term Bible.) Only the pure in heart can stand against the temptations of the evil one. Only the pure in heart can live a life that will measure up to the standards of God's Word. Only one person has a pure heart, and that is Jesus. He wants to live in us, and give us His heart. We are the temple of God.

The pure in heart are going to see God face to face. Satan will be dealt with and the dead will be judged. Everything will be made new! There will be a new heaven and a new earth. The New Jerusalem, the bride of Christ, will come down out of heaven. The abode of God will be among men.

"And there shall in no wise enter into it anything unclean or that works abomination or makes a lie, but only those who are written in the Lamb's book of life.

And he showed me a pure river of water of life, clear as crystal, proceeding out of the throne of God and of the Lamb. In the midst of her plaza and on either side of the river was the tree of life, which brings forth twelve manner of fruits, yielding her fruit every month; and the leaves of the tree are for the healing of the Gentiles. **And there shall no longer be any cursed thing;...** " (Revelation 21:27-22:3)

This is the end result of the Beatitudes. The river of life, flows from God's throne. Redeemed and regenerate humanity has regained access to the tree of life, the healing of the nations will follow. God's blessing has overcome the curse. God's Battle Plan has succeeded in overcoming the enemy and an eternity of peace is on the horizon. Contrast this with our "modern" cities that generate pollution, misery and despair.

"And there shall no longer be any cursed thing; but the throne of God and of the Lamb shall be in her; and his servants shall serve him; and they shall see his face; and his name shall be in their foreheads. And there shall be no night there; and they need no lamp neither light of the sun; for the Lord God shall give them light; and they shall reign for ever and ever." (Revelation 22:3-5)

The seventh Beatitude:

"Blessed are the peacemakers, for they shall be called the sons of God."

The seventh line of the Lord's Prayer:

"For thine is the kingdom and the power and the glory forever. Amen."

The seventh Beatitude in Revelation:

"Blessed are those who do his commandments that their power and authority might be in the tree of life and they may enter in through the gates into the city."
(Revelation 22:14)

The sons of God shall inherit the kingdom. They are joint heirs with Jesus Christ. Our robes must be washed in the blood of the Lamb. We must die daily to our own plans and ambitions and live for Him if we are to have power and authority in the tree of life and truly be able to administer God's peace to those who do not have it.

"But outside are the dogs and the sorcerers and the fornicators and the murderers and the idolaters and whosoever loves and makes a lie.

I, Jesus, have sent my angel to testify unto you these things in the churches. I AM the root and the offspring of David and the bright and morning star.

And the Spirit and the bride say, Come. And let him that hears say, Come. And let him that is thirsty come; and whosoever will, let him take of the water of life freely." (Revelation 22:15-17)